Nine Lives
The Story of Biggin Hill

NINE LIVES

THE STORY OF BIGGIN HILL

Alex Martin

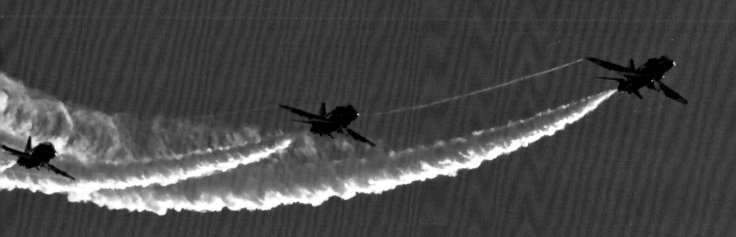

UNICORN

Published in 2023 by Unicorn
an imprint of Unicorn Publishing Group LLP
Charleston Studio
Meadow Business Centre
Lewes BN8 5RW
www.unicornpublishing.org

ISBN 978-1-914414-15-2

10 9 8 7 6 5 4 3 2 1

Designed by Anikst Design.London
Printed in the UK by Gomer Press, Wales

Contents

Foreword
Air Chief Marshal Sir Michael Graydon GCB CBE FRAeS

Airfields are spread across the United Kingdom. A number were established in World War I, but most in World War II when the crucial contribution to the war that aviation would provide was responsible for the massive increase in their number.

Every airfield or Station has a personality; it arises from its location, its tasks and the people who lived and served there. Today many lie derelict, re-brigaded or built over; but the men and women whose lives were so closely bound up with their base will remember a special relationship with great affection.

There are just a few airfields that have survived the last tumultuous 100 years and have thrived on a wider stage. Biggin Hill is at the head of this distinguished group.

The history of this iconic Royal Air Force Station and its residents, so well described by Alex Martin, provides a clue as to how this has been achieved; it lies in the ability to reinvent itself.

From its birth in World War I, through the years of decay and reformation up to World War II, the airfield was home to a variety of military roles all of which led to a base well prepared for war and by its location destined to play a major part in the defence of the nation and its capital.

In the Battle of Britain, the name of Biggin Hill resounded around the world; it took the stage for 'The Few' — the pilots of the Battle of Britain — and for the magnificent groundcrew and supporting military agencies. It represented the nation's resilience and courage in resisting the Nazi scourge. It was a foundational moment in the Station's life.

Post-war it continued to reinvent itself in a variety of important military roles, merger with civilian operators, acclaimed air shows, continual struggles with Ministries and at times with the local Council, to where it is today, a highly successful civilian enterprise for aviation and other business activities — all this achieved despite the immense challenges of the post-war period.

What has been the secret? It is of course an ingredient that has been at the heart of Biggin Hill throughout its life: its leaders and their vision, energy and people skills. A host of great Royal Air Force leaders, many of whom achieved the highest ranks in war and peace; post-war, and in the fight for survival, commercial people such as Jock Maitland and Edward Drewery whose tenacity was crucial in the battle with state bureaucracy. More recently, Andrew Walters and then his son Robert, whose business acumen and specialist experience have been instrumental in consolidating Biggin Hill as the go-to business airport and specialist national and international aviation hub. A diversity of enterprise with high quality premises and management offers impressive prospects for the future, and it is to the credit of them all that the superb youth organisation of Air Cadets has continued to thrive at the airfield.

Air Chief Marshal Sir Michael Graydon

These remarkable men all understood the importance of team work, in recruiting 'The Right Stuff' and in the creation of a family culture. When people look forward to going to work each day as is evident at Biggin Hill then something special is at hand.

I could not complete this Foreword without a mention of Simon Ames whose establishment and oversight of the renowned International Air Fair at 'The Bump', which ran from 1963 to 2018, was so influential. In the risk-averse world in which we seem to live, air shows are, as described by Alex Martin, an endangered species. Yet, as countless surveys have shown, the public loves them, they are a platform for British aviation and skill, and they have influenced many young men and women to enter a career in aviation. Memories of The Biggin Hill International Air Fair are yet another feature in the gleaming tapestry of this famous and flourishing airfield.

CHAPTER 1
THE BIRTH OF AN AIRFIELD
1917–18

O n an autumn day in 1916, two young officers in the Royal Flying Corps, Lt Hansard and Lt Furnival, drove into the Kent countryside to look for a suitable site for a new airfield. They were stationed at Joyce Green, near Dartford, an Army airstrip at the confluence of two rivers, the Darent and Thames. Joyce Green presented dangers and obstacles on all sides, with a sewage works, an explosives factory and the waters of the rivers lying in wait for unwary pilots: 29 of them died there and are commemorated in a local church. It was particularly inhospitable in winter, with waterlogged ground and frequent fogs.[1]

Still, Joyce Green was an important place: the home of the Wireless Testing Park, where the Army carried out experiments on the use of radio in aviation.

Radio was a new technology at that time, almost as new as powered flight. Guglielmo Marconi sent the first radio signal across the Atlantic in December 1901, two years before the Wright Brothers took their historic first flight at Kitty Hawk. Both radio and aviation had developed quickly since then, accelerated by the demands of war. By 1914 aeroplanes were already playing an important part on the battlefield, in reconnaissance, photography, artillery observation and contact patrols (helping commanders stay in touch with their troops). Communication was awkward — by flares and other visual signals from the ground, by klaxons and message streamers from the air; also, more swiftly, by wireless telegraphy, using morse code. The process of keying in a sequence of dots and dashes for each letter or number, however, was laborious and distracting, especially for a pilot trying to fly over enemy lines and avoid being shot down. Communication by voice, using radio telephony, would be an obvious improvement, but, despite intensive research by radio engineers at Brooklands, Woolwich and Joyce Green, no satisfactory results had yet been achieved. Experiments at the Wireless Testing Park had to go on throughout the year, and in all weathers. With winter approaching, the search for an alternative site to Joyce Green became pressing.

One of the officers, Douglas Hansard, had been brought up in Limpsfield, on the Kent-Surrey border, and knew of a place that might fit the bill: a flat expanse of farmland south of Bromley, high up on the Downs, in the parish of Cudham. It occupied an area between the hamlets of Biggin Hill, Leaves Green and Downe, bounded by the Westerham-Bromley road to the west and a strip of woodland to the east (See map overleaf). Cudham Lodge farmhouse lay just off-centre, but there were plenty of open fields around it. The site was already designated as an emergency landing ground. Its owner, Earl Stanhope of Chevening, was a military man and keen to help.[2]

Stanhope and his tenant farmer, John Westacott, made way for the Royal Flying Corps in December 1916, renting out 178 acres of land. Teams of labourers set to work levelling the site, erecting tents, huts and canvas hangars, while negotiations began for the acquisition of a house on the western edge of the site for an Officers' Mess. This house, nam ed 'Koonowla', belonged to the Victoria Hospital for Sick Children and was

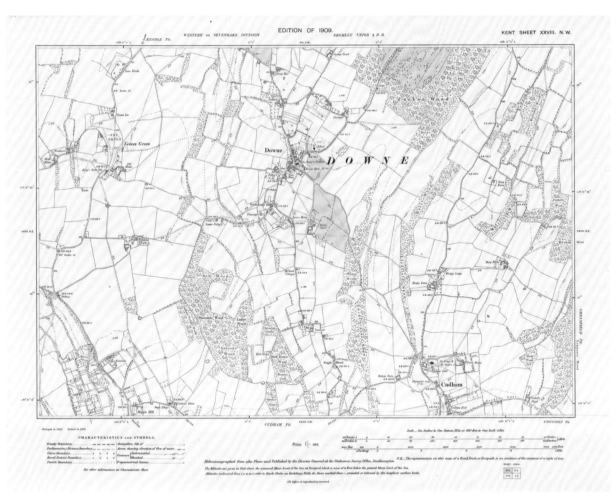

in use as a convalescent home for its poorest patients. The trustees were far from keen to surrender it, but when the War Office invoked the Defence of the Realm Act of 1914 they had little choice.

The first aeroplane to land at Biggin Hill was an RE 7, flown by Lieutenant Dickie, with Air Mechanic Chadwick as his passenger. As they rolled towards the hangar they were pelted with snowballs. Dickie and Chadwick kissed the ground as they stepped down. The date was 2nd January 1917.

As more aircraft, stores and equipment moved in, the Army engineers got to work on a series of technical challenges: building suitable transmitters and receivers, with simple switches and controls easy to operate while flying an aeroplane; making leather flying helmets with stitched-in headsets; rigging up aerials — on the ground and on aircraft; devising a simple, unambiguous language for radio communication; providing fixed radio beacons for navigation; testing radio equipment and procedures in the air, at various distances and heights, and in all weathers.

Living conditions were harsh that winter: tents or wooden huts for accommodation, with aircraft packing cases turned into makeshift offices and workshops. The transfer of the Wireless Testing Park was completed by 13th February. Major-General Trenchard, who commanded the Royal Flying Corps, had issued clear requirements for aircraft radios: a one-mile range all round, no adjustments to the transmitter when in use, and only one tuning movement allowed on the receiver; total reliability of the

equipment, perfect speech quality, and a maximum aerial length of 150 feet, to be superseded by a fixed aerial if possible.

Various types of aerial were tried: one was a reel of copper wire with a weight on the end, unwound once airborne and trailed through the sky, but often forgotten, only to catch in trees or other obstacles as the aircraft came in to land. Another type was the 'fixed aerial', a length of wire laid inside a wing. A radio set developed in 1915 by the Marconi company at Brooklands (the Round-Prince) produced the best results, but clear transmission of speech was not achieved until July 1917, when two crews in Sopwith 1½-Strutters (Lts Hansard and Andrews in one, Peck[3] and Furnival in the other) managed to communicate on a sunset flight over Sevenoaks and Edenbridge. The message from Andrews was nothing more exciting than the numbers 1 to 10 and the days of the week, acknowledged by Furnival's aircraft dipping its wings — but the moment was a turning point.

They were invited to demonstrate their results to Trenchard and the Air Staff in France. After the demonstration, an order was immediately placed for twenty aircraft to be equipped with radio sets. Furnival returned to France to equip and train 11

Squadron in their Bristol Fighters. He was then asked to set up a school of wireless telephony at Biggin Hill.

A second demonstration was staged for the King and a group of generals at Horse Guards Parade in London, with aircraft from Biggin Hill performing a mock attack on St Paul's Cathedral, intercepting an 'enemy raider' over Crystal Palace, and flying a sequence of aerobatics — all following radio instructions given by the Flight Commander. The King and the generals watched the display with fascination and listened to the radio exchanges on a special receiving set.

In the summer and autumn of 1917, Biggin Hill received nine new BE 2e aircraft, a proper all-metal hangar, a team of wireless operator instructors, and the services of a former professional singer, Lt Gooch, as a voice coach. Each week 36 officers passed through the school. It was a popular posting, being conveniently near to London and the entertainments of the West End.

Meanwhile Trenchard was considering a new problem. What if the enemy captured a radio-equipped aeroplane and eavesdropped on battlefield communications? If this happened, it was imperative the enemy should not understand what was being said. So Biggin Hill staff were also tasked with inventing a code, to be instantly understood by those in the know but baffling to outsiders. Experiments led to the conclusion that two-syllable words were less ambiguous than one, and short double words like 'dog-rose' or 'shot-gun' were best of all. Important military messages were disguised with nonsensical and humorous phrases of a kind that were amusing to a generation brought up on Edward Lear and Lewis Carroll, but were pure gobbledygook to a listening German. Terms such as 'pancake' for an emergency landing, 'angels' for altitude (an angel was equivalent to 1,000 feet), 'bandit' for enemy aircraft and colourful names for squadron commanders are all familiar from films about the Battle of Britain, but this innocent-sounding language had its origins in the First World War. The code word for Biggin Hill was 'Dollars'.

At the end of 1917, the Wireless Testing Park was renamed the Wireless Experimental Establishment, and Aperfield Court, a large house on high ground two miles south of the airfield, was requisitioned. Wireless workshops were set up inside, together with a powerful transmitter for ground-to-air control of fighters defending London from aerial attack (see 'The Defence of London', below).

On 1st April 1918 the Royal Air Force was formally established and all wireless research for the new service was concentrated at Biggin Hill. Staff were transferred from other establishments, notably the Royal Naval Air Service Experimental Establishment at Cranwell and the Army's Signals Experimental Establishment at Woolwich. Lieutenant Colonel L. F. Blandy, previously in charge of Wireless for the Army in France, was appointed Officer Commanding, with another radio engineer, Basil Binyon, as his director of research. Staff numbers grew to 68 officers, 297 men and 228 women.

IT IS FAR BETTER
TO FACE THE BULLETS
THAN TO BE KILLED
AT HOME BY A BOMB

JOIN THE ARMY AT ONCE
& HELP TO STOP AN AIR RAID

GOD SAVE THE KING

opposite (upper)
A Royal Aircraft Factory BE 2e, one of the first fighter aircraft stationed at Biggin Hill for the defence of London in December 1917.

opposite (lower)
A Bristol Fighter at Biggin Hill in 1918. Captain Manning is the pilot and Captain Andrews the observer-gunner-wireless operator. Below the roundel one can see the aerial with a weight on the end, which would be unreeled during flight.

above right
A British Government poster of 1915.

Biggin Hill's facilities were improved with the further development of the South Camp. This was the area designated for the Wireless Experimental Establishment's workshops, hangars, laboratories, messes, medical facilities and barracks. A budget of £220,000 and a civilian workforce of more than 600 were assigned to the construction, which was expected to take two years.

Runways (all grass until the first concrete runway was laid in 1940) were lengthened to take twin-engined bombers — De Havilland DH 10s and Handley Page 0/400s. More land was requisitioned, including a nearby fruit farm. The farmer, according to one eye-witness, was 'in a highly indignant state as acres and acres of luscious strawberries were to be destroyed, and was given a few days to pick what he could. He asked permission to enrol Service personnel as pickers. I have never seen such a rush of volunteers for a fatigue party!'[4]

The Defence of London

German bombing raids on Britain, aimed at terrorising the population, began in December 1914 — first with seaplanes, then with airships known as 'Zeppelins' after their most famous manufacturer and pioneer, Graf Ferdinand von Zeppelin. Airships had been developed before the war for luxury travel, with cabins, viewing lounges and cocktail bars, but were rather less suitable as bombers. They tended to be blown

off course by unruly winds, and often dropped their bombs in the wrong places; British seaside towns took a nasty battering. Being filled with hydrogen, the Zeppelins were also vulnerable to machine gun fire, particularly when the guns were loaded with incendiary or explosive ammunition. Of the 84 airships used in a total of 51 raids, 30 were destroyed by fighter aircraft or in accidents.

In 1917 the Germans began using aeroplanes to drop bombs, twin-engined Gothas and 'Giants' (Zeppelin-Staakens).[5] These were much harder to spot and shoot down than airships. A total of 8,578 bombs were dropped on Britain during the war, killing 1,414, injuring 3,416 and causing extensive damage to buildings. A daylight raid by 21 Gothas struck Folkestone in 1917, killing 56 women and children in a shopping street. On 13th June 1917 the first daytime raid on London caused 162 deaths and 432 injuries. Although 92 fighter aeroplanes took to the air that day in London's defence, not a single German bomber was shot down.

In response to this campaign of terror, German cities, ports and military installations were targeted by British bombers. A ring of defences was also set up around London. Searchlights, sound locators, observation posts, anti-aircraft batteries, barrage balloons and squadrons of fighter aircraft were strategically placed at aerodromes in the suburbs and counties of Kent and Essex. Biggin Hill, south-east of London, lay directly in the bombers' path. On 1st December 1917 it became an operational fighter station.

Two Bessonneau hangars, made from timber and canvas, with room for four aircraft in each, were erected in the snow near the Salt Box (see map); these were the beginnings of Biggin Hill's North Camp. Six BE 2e and BE 12 aircraft, which made up 'D' Flight from 39 Squadron, flew in from Hornchurch. The aeroplanes went into one hangar, the officers into the other. The hangars, even with tents pitched inside, gave poor protection from the freezing weather. The officers were moved into Armstrong huts — cheap, quickly assembled, timber-framed structures resembling long garden sheds, with asbestos walls and corrugated steel or timber cladding. Armstrong huts

left
A Zeppelin-Staaken R VI bomber, known as a 'Giant', used in nocturnal raids on London in 1917–18.

opposite (upper)
Hangars and huts typical of British airfields in the First World War. The two canvas structures in the centre are Bessonneau hangars. To the left, Armstrong huts, to the right a more permanent hangar. (Photograph taken at Spittlegate, Lincolnshire, but Biggin Hill had similar buildings.)

opposite (lower)
Headquarters hut, Wireless Testing Park, Biggin Hill 1917.

were erected in their thousands during the war, on military bases at home and abroad. They were unhealthy buildings to live in, but no one was expected to stay very long.

The first fighter sortie was flown at 4am on the night of 7th-8th December 1917. An L-shaped flare path was laid out with canisters of cotton waste soaked in paraffin and set alight (the long arm laid in the direction of the wind, the short arm at right angles to it, indicating where to stop). Three BE 12s took off into the moonlit sky to patrol the area between Biggin Hill and the Thames. Searchlights probed the darkness, but the six German raiders dropped their deadly loads and made off without being seen. Cecil Lewis describes flying on these missions, 'peering through the night trying to spot the black silhouette of an enemy, but it was futile; like trying to see a fly in a dark room'.[6] Two German aeroplanes were hit by gunfire from the ground, but none by Home Defence aircraft. The fighters returned to base. On 22nd December two more German raids took place and the fighters went up again, without result. It was all very frustrating.

Meanwhile the weather deteriorated. Six-foot snowdrifts blocked the Westerham to Bromley road and the Armstrong huts were declared uninhabitable. Crown Ash

left
A recruiting poster of 1918.

above
Crown Ash Cottage, used as an Officers' Mess in 1918.

opposite
Hardit Singh Malik, a young Indian officer in the Royal Flying Corps. He was stationed at Biggin Hill in 1918 between tours of duty in France. This photograph was taken at Balliol College, Oxford, where he was studying History at the start of the First World War.

Cottage, opposite the Salt Box, was requisitioned as an Officers' Mess and the fighter pilots settled in. The farmer at Cudham Lodge, John Westacott, and his wife Edith made everyone welcome. A local girl, Sybil Holden, recalled, 'My sisters and I, being musical, were sometimes invited to Cudham Lodge, and many of the young pilots would come to supper. I well remember how these visits were saddened by the high rate of mortality among these fine young men.'

One morning in January, Crown Ash Cottage rang with cries of alarm. A batman carrying hot water to the officers was terrified to find a dark man with a beard and turban asleep in one of the beds. This turned out to be 23-year-old Hardit Singh Malik — one of only four Indians to serve with the Royal Flying Corps in the First World War. Malik was a student at Oxford when war broke out, a brilliant cricketer and golfer, and a contemporary of Harold Macmillan. 'Everyone at Oxford began to join up,' he said. 'All my friends went. It seemed such an adventure. But when I tried to get into the army I was told there were no vacancies for Indian students.'[7]

Malik insisted on playing his part. He volunteered as an ambulance driver for the French Red Cross, carrying wounded and sick from the Western Front to a hospital in south-west France. He then applied to the French Air Force and was accepted for pilot training. At once his tutor at Oxford, Francis Urqhuart, wrote an indignant letter to General Sir David Henderson, Commander of the Royal Flying Corps in France, saying that if Malik was good enough for the French he was surely good enough for the British. Malik was invited to join the service. He learned to fly at RFC Filton and was posted to 28 Squadron in Flanders. He flew a number of missions, culminating in a lonely encounter with four German fighters over enemy territory. Having run out of ammunition, with bullets smashing into his aeroplane and his legs, he turned for home and, faint from loss of blood, crash-landed in the shell-cratered landscape behind Allied lines. He was pulled out of his cockpit unconscious. 'The strange thing was,' he writes, 'that while in the first few moments I felt sure I would be killed or at least shot down and captured, and that did not happen, I felt quite calm and confident, believing that I was under divine protection, and would escape. My pursuers just did not have the bullet with my name on it.'[8]

After the War, Malik joined the Indian Civil Service. His posts included Trade Commissioner in the USA, Prime Minister of Patiala, High Commissioner in Canada, and Ambassador to France. He was a popular figure at Biggin Hill, breezy and good-natured, yet strongly principled and not afraid to speak his mind.

Malik tells this revealing story in his autobiography: 'While at Biggin Hill I was detailed to fly to France with three pilots and hand over four planes which were required urgently to replace planes lost in severe fighting to the base at St Omer. Major Baker was commanding our squadron. He later became Air Marshal Sir Brian Baker. He was an extraordinary man, most efficient, with a tremendous sense of humour, a strict

A Sopwith Camel at Biggin Hill in 1918. Flt Sgt Draper (centre) and Cpl Chadwick (behind him) are the only named figures in this RAF photograph.

and just disciplinarian, yet with a sweet disposition. He put me in charge of the party and told us that after handing over our planes to the CO at St Omer, we were to fly back to England in a large Handley Page used to ferry pilots between England and France. We watched this aircraft land at St Omer after we had handed over the planes. The Handley Page did not have a good reputation and I did not like the way the pilot, with whom we were supposed to return, handled the plane. As the officer in charge of the party, I took the responsibility of telling the CO at St Omer that we could not fly back with that pilot as I did not consider it safe. The CO was furious but couldn't do much about it. So we returned to England by boat. At Biggin Hill that evening Baker informed me that he had received orders from the General to put me under arrest for disobeying the CO's orders at St Omer. I explained my reason for refusing the orders and Baker told me I had done well for he had just heard that the same Handley Page had crashed on landing at Lympne and everyone in it had been killed. In spite of this I was to consider myself under arrest until the General countermanded his orders. But Baker indicated that this was a mere formality and I was free to go where I liked, which gave me a chance for pleasure flying, including a visit to my old golf club at Eastbourne. The old members were excited when I landed on my old school football field alongside the golf course.'[9]

On 8th February 1918, with permanent buildings now going up in the North Camp, Biggin Hill became home to 141 Squadron, formed a few weeks before at Rochford in Essex. At the same time, No 17 Anti-Aircraft Company of the Royal Engineers moved in with equipment, stores, a pay office and telephonists. They operated 16 searchlight stations in the northwest Kent area, working closely with gun sites. One of their officers, Lt Bellman, remembered that the machines in use at Biggin Hill were 'constantly changing — BEs, FEs (pusher planes), Avros, Bristol Fighters (the main wing), a Martinsyde, Handley Page, etc. A few Fokkers were "imported" for practice flying and investigation.'

A more complete air defence system was now created, with an Operations Room organised by the dynamic Lieutenant Furnival. Information from the Coast Guard, anti-aircraft gun sites and the Metropolitan Observer Service was co-ordinated here and relayed to the pilots of 141, allowing them to react more swiftly to incoming raids.

The first 'kill' by a fighter from Biggin Hill was achieved on the night of 19th–20th May 1918, when Lt EE Turner (pilot) and Lt HB Barwise (observer), flying a Bristol Fighter, attacked a Gotha that was heading home after bombing Rotherhithe and Peckham. Despite being riddled with bullets, the Gotha kept going. It was hit again by another fighter, a Sopwith Camel flown by Major Sowrey of 143 Squadron, before crashing at Harrietsham, a few miles southeast of Maidstone. There was some uncertainty about who should be credited with its destruction. Eventually the German gunner, the sole survivor of the crash, confirmed that the first attack had been decisive. Turner and Barwise both received the Distinguished Flying Cross.

This turned out to be the last major air raid on London in the First World War. Faced with fuel shortages and ever more effective air defences, the German bombing campaign was called off.

The summer of 1918 was a listless time for 141 Squadron, with little fighting to do. Their commanding officer, Major Baker, countered their boredom with daily rugby matches and more challenging work, such as tight formation flying, 'wing-tip inside wing-tip'. Not quite 22 years old when he took command on 1st July 1918, Baker had fought brilliantly on the Western Front, shooting down 12 enemy aircraft between June and November 1917. He was awarded the Military Cross, the Distinguished Service Order and the Croix de Guerre. His DSO citation stated, 'his work on all occasions has been magnificent. He is a dashing patrol leader, and inspires all with the greatest keenness.'

His men were young and high-spirited. 'We used to get very bored flying around all morning in formation,' recalled Norman Dimmock, 'so to pass the time we would pretend to be a band. I would brace up in the front seat and tap the wing prior to conducting, and everyone would go through the motions of playing one instrument or other.'[10] Nocturnal japes included stealing clocks from the Wireless Establishment's aircraft, capturing a giant wooden teapot that hung outside a tea-room in the village, hi-jacking a steam-roller, breaking windows and trashing the mess piano.

Foolish and drunken as some of this behaviour was, it had its own wartime logic. Just like the next generation, who would fight in the Battle of Britain, these young men lived intensely, in the shadow of death. Their existence was an enervating blend of violence and boredom. Their average life expectancy in combat was three weeks. If enemy action did not kill them, there was a good chance that engine failure would. Frivolity was a way of coping with fear, anxiety and the daily disappearance of friends.

The playful spirit had a heroic side too, a refusal to be broken by the war, which one can sense in the black humour of a 'requiem', sung by the pilots when a comrade was killed:

A brave aviator lay dying
And as on his deathbed he lay,
To his swearing mechanics around him
These last dying words did he say:

Take the cylinder out of my kidneys,
The connecting rod out of my brain,
From the small of my back take the gearbox
And assemble the engine again.

So gather up quickly the fragments
And when you've returned them to store,
Write a letter to Seely and tell him
His 141st is no more.

When the Court of Enquiry assembles,
Please tell them the reason I died,
Was because I forgot twice iota
Was the maximum angle of glide.

So when I am dead I'll be joining
The Flying Corps up in the sky.
Let's hope that they've studied iota,
And the wings that they give me will fly![11]

In the summer of 1918, to keep up the fighter pilots' morale and sharpen their appetite for excellence, a Squadron-at-Arms Competition was devised by Brigadier-General TCR Higgins, the General Commanding the VIth (London Defence) Brigade. After preliminary rounds and inspections of airfields, the final event was to be held at Sutton's Farm in Essex on 22nd September: a gala occasion with over 100 aeroplanes and a host of distinguished guests, including the Minister for Air, Lord Weir. Squadrons were awarded points for formation flying, aerobatics, target shooting, wireless telephony, and a *concours d'élégance* to include not only aircraft but also the upkeep and appearance of their home stations.

Biggin Hill's 141, galvanised by a sudden urge to do well, laboured hard through September to spruce up the airfield and its buildings, clearing debris, planting trees, and laying lawns with neat white stone verges. When the great day came, they were outdone in the first two events: formation flying and the race to get airborne from a klaxon signal. High hopes rested on their marksman, Lt Langford-Sainsbury, in the gunnery event. Langford-Sainsbury put in a dazzling performance, and now 141 were in the lead. The final test, for proficiency in wireless telephony, required six aircraft from each squadron to write down the words of a message transmitted from Aperfield Court. As neighbours of the Wireless Experimental Establishment, 141 felt confident — perhaps too confident. General Higgins noted this, and set them a fiendishly difficult extract from that day's *Times*:

> The Japanese military attaché in London has received information to the effect that Blakovestshesk and Alexeievsk were occupied by Japanese cavalry covering from Khabarovsk and Tsitsikhar on 18th September.

To everyone's amazement — and disbelief — this text was noted down perfectly by the men of 141. Higgins suspected a trick and ordered another test. Again 141 achieved near perfection. They won the day, and with it a silver cup, the name 'Cock Squadron' and the right to paint a crimson and gold cockerel on their aeroplanes.

In the autumn of 1918 Biggin Hill achieved another first, when a Handley Page 0/400 bomber flew to Paris on a day of thick cloud, navigating entirely by radio direction finding (RDF) with no visual clues from the ground. The system, developed by the Wireless Experimental Establishment, permitted a base station to track an aircraft's position and send a signal known as a QDM (Q code Direction Magnetic) indicating a course for the pilot to steer.

Successes like this were the fruit of hard work. In 1918 the WEE inspected a total of 6,810 pieces of apparatus, including 2,967 microphones, 737 wireless receivers for aircraft, 705 remote controls, 443 transmitters, and 326 generators. Of all items, 5,480 passed and 1,330 were rejected, although many of the rejects were adjusted and sub-

left (upper)
Biggin Hill's first fighter Squadron, 141, after their triumph in the Squadron-at-Arms Competition, 22nd September 1918. Their commanding officer, Major Brian Baker, holds the trophy for air gunnery which they have just won. The officer to his right is in charge of the squadron's new mascot, a cock.

left (lower)
'The Cock Squadron', 141, in triumph, 22nd September 1918.

right
The visit of the Japanese Prince Admiral Yorihito, autumn 1918.

sequently passed. The report for the year states that 'Research work during the war was to a considerable extent retarded by the necessity for rapid production of sets for the Services,' but a good deal of research and investigation was carried out, 'chiefly with regard to valve characteristics, the self-oscillation of valves, and the elimination of magneto disturbances.' This was in addition to the 'design of new apparatus or modification of existing sets to meet the needs of the fighting forces, improvements in Radio-Telephony and experiments in two-way working, experimental work in Direction Finding, and experimental work with Fixed Aerials and Tank Aerials.'

For the last of these, the engineers had a tank at their disposal, but as the report cannily phrased it, 'a considerable amount of ingenuity was necessary before the exacting conditions for this type of aerial could be met.' In fact they were not met, but this was passed over in silence.

By the end of the war, Biggin Hill was an enormous establishment, fully equipped and staffed as both a research and fighter station. Photographs of the time show officers and men posing formally or competing in sports events. We also see convoys of lorries, motorcycles, fighters, bombers and transport aircraft, and some permanent buildings. The aerodrome's proximity to London and its pioneering work in radio was already making it a favoured destination for official visits. In the autumn of 1918 the Japanese Prince Admiral Higashi Fushimi Yorihito was given a tour, attended by impeccably attired senior officers of both Navy and Air Force, with a solid-looking hangar to shelter them from the rain.

The Armistice of 11th November 1918 triggered wild celebrations. Graham Wallace tells the story that 'a drowsy wireless operator at Aperfield Court, with nothing better to do, tuned into the Eiffel Tower station and picked up the message:

"Marshal Foch to C-in-Cs:

"Hostilities will cease on the whole Front as from Nov 11th at 11 o'clock (French time)."

'The excited operator told Colonel Blandy who passed on the tidings to Major Baker and the local padres. In a few minutes the bells of Cudham and Westerham were pealing merrily, the first in all Britain to proclaim the end of hostilities.'

The farmer from Cudham Lodge, John Westacott, galloped into the Officers' Mess on horseback and rode around the billiard table in exultation. 'The Wireless Flight pilots brought out their aircraft and gave joy-rides to all the girls in Biggin Hill. Both Blandy and Baker announced a day's leave for all and soon everyone was heading towards the West End.'

A party burst into the Savoy Hotel and called for champagne at 10 in the morning. Officers from 141 Squadron 'exuberantly dragged the guns in Hyde Park down the Mall and left them lying under Admiralty Arch. In the Strand they climbed on the roof of a taxi caught in the crowds and danced until it collapsed. Then they drove to the Criterion and jammed the taxi in the entrance where it burst into flames.... Later that night the two units from Biggin Hill, the fighter pilots and the wireless officers, had a rendezvous at the Savoy. They took over the band and formed a wild crocodile dancing through and over the tables reserved for generals and "red tabs". An elderly guest, watching the fun with a tolerant eye, enjoyed himself so much that he footed the bill for all the broken crockery and glass.' Small wonder that 'next day London was out of bounds to all officers and other ranks.'

Meanwhile in France, Flt Lt Malik, now with 11 Squadron at Aulnoye, 'had a really rough night of it, with much shouting, singing, shooting off Very lights, coloured flares...'

left
Blanche Castle (left) and Christine Nelson, locally recruited as typists for the Women's Royal Air Force at Biggin Hill. Picture by William Nelson, who had a photographic studio in the village. His work is a valuable record of its lives and buildings from 1900 to 1926..

above
Motor Transport personnel posing in front of a Leyland lorry, Biggin Hill 1918.

opposite
A private billet at Biggin Hill in 1917. The RFC airmen in the picture are named as (back row) Brookes, Howarth, Gibbons, (front) Stott, Jepson. The names of their hosts are unknown.

Yet one haunting scene stayed with him: 'an infantry battalion returning from the trenches marching past our airfield at Aulnoye, totally exhausted, covered with mud, some of them still bloody with slight wounds, half asleep as they walked on. They showed no reaction to the Armistice, too fed up and weary to care — a great contrast to the boisterous spirit of the RAF personnel that day.'

1   The memorial is in St Alban's Church, Dartford. For photographs and further details of Joyce Green, see Peter Osborne, *RAF Biggin Hill, The Other Side of the Bump*, Chapter 2.
2   James Richard Stanhope, 7th Earl Stanhope KG DSO MC PC (1880-1967), soldier and politician.
3   He would later be Air Marshal Sir Richard Peck.
4   W. Wallis, quoted in Graham Wallace, *RAF Biggin Hill*, 25-6.
5   There is some remarkable ciné footage of this aircraft in *German 'Giant' Over London: The Zeppelin-Staaken R.VI, 1917–18* (Mark Felton Productions), which can be found on YouTube.
6   Cecil Lewis, *Sagittarius Rising*, Chapter 5
7   Michael Partridge, 'The Flying Sikh - Hardit Singh Malik', *The Old Eastbournian* (2000)
8   Hardit Singh Malik, *A Little Work, A Little Play*, 88
9   Hardit Singh Malik, *A Little Work, A Little Play*, 94–5
10 Norman Herford Dimmock AFC (1898-1980). His high spirits and piano-playing while serving with 46 Squadron in France during the summer of 1917 are vividly described by Arthur Gould Lee in his book *No Parachute*.
11 Quoted in Wallace, page 45. Seely was Major-General Seely, Under Secretary of Sate for Air. 'Iota' is the square root of -1, an imaginary number.

CHAPTER 2
BETWEEN THE WARS
1919–39

O nce the peace celebrations were over, a time of reckoning began. The War had left families without fathers and sons, governments deeply in debt, and millions of people without jobs. The army that had fought and endured infernal conditions for four years in France returned to a promise from Lloyd George to 'make Britain a fit country for heroes to live in'. Like many a political promise this one turned out to be hollow, since public spending had to be tightly controlled after the financial haemorrhage of the War. Typically a year of war costs ten times as much as a year of peace.

Trouble was now brewing all over Europe as traditional ways of thinking were questioned and old empires collapsed. Regimes were overthrown in Russia, Germany, Hungary, Turkey, Italy and Ireland. Even Biggin Hill had its episode of unrest, when the deprivations of war continued too long into the peace. In his book *RAF Biggin Hill*, which was based on numerous eyewitness accounts, Graham Wallace described the scene at the airfield in December 1919: 'Living conditions at the South Camp were appalling. The civilian contractors had demolished most of the wooden huts but were doing little to replace them. An atmosphere of apathy and post-war inertia hung over the site and some 500 men were compelled in midwinter to live under canvas, or in the few leaking, indescribably filthy huts that remained. They had no baths, no heating, nowhere to wash and dry clothes. It rained unceasingly, a canvas Bessonneau hangar with its roof in tatters served as a dining hall, the benches and tables were saturated and stood in three inches of mud. The kitchen was an open shed of rusting iron some yards away. All duck boards had long been burnt as fuel and orderlies had to slither ankle-deep through mud, often falling, food and all, into the morass.'[1]

The men of the Wireless Experimental Establishment had often complained, without receiving a satisfactory response. In January 1919 they decided to go on strike. They refused to report for duty and presented the Commanding Officer, Colonel Blandy, with a list of demands. This was technically a mutiny, but Blandy knew the grievances were legitimate and offered to accompany a delegation to the General Commanding the South-East Area. The General reacted angrily to this act of insubordination and refused to meet them, but his second-in-command, Brigadier-General ACH McLean, offered to mediate. He toured the South Camp and was shocked at what he saw. The civilian contractors were called in and, after some hard bargaining, were persuaded to make all necessary improvements within ten days. McLean announced: 'The entire station will go on leave from noon today, but don't expect to find a "Hotel Savoy" on your return.'

A vote of thanks was passed and the men returned to discipline. Travel warrants were issued with the help of volunteers and by the end of the day the South Camp was empty. Ten days later the accommodation had been greatly improved and the trouble was over. 'All in all,' says Wallace, 'it was a very gentlemanly mutiny.'[2]

In 1919 the Air Ministry decided, in the interests of economy, to reorganise the work of the RAF's experimental establishments. Research into signals, wireless, instruments,

previous page
Pilots and Bristol Bulldogs of 32 Squadron at a
flight-line briefing, RAF Biggin Hill, 1934.

left (upper)
The Avro 504K, used for instrument
testing at Biggin Hill after the First
World War.

left (lower)
Men from the Instrument Design
Establishment, Biggin Hill, outside the
House of Lords for a demonstration of
wireless telephony, August 1919.

right
Major-General Jack Seely, Under-
Secretary for Air in 1919, a keen supporter
of the experiments in radio at Biggin Hill.

navigation and meteorology was to be concentrated at one station. Biggin Hill was
chosen, and the WEE was renamed the Instrument Design Establishment (IDE). Staff
numbers were cut from almost 600 to 346, of whom 142 were civilians. Their task: to
keep Britain at the leading edge of aeronautical instrument design and to provide the
RAF with the best equipment available. Five pilots were assigned to IDE, test-flying
instruments in Avro 504s. Meanwhile 'Cock' Squadron, 141, was transferred to Tallaght
in Ireland in March 1919, to be replaced by 39 Squadron, equipped with Sopwith
Camels, from Stow Maries in Essex.

In August 1919, the Under-Secretary for Air, Maj-Gen Jack Seely, one of the more
flamboyant military men of his generation, arranged a demonstration of the powers
of wireless technology for a group of MPs, Peers, Treasury officials and high-ranking
RAF officers. They gathered in the House of Lords. With a radio set in front of him,
Seely contacted the Wireless Officer at Aperfield Court, near Biggin Hill, who recited
a short poem and played Tchaikovsky's 1812 Overture on the gramophone. The audience
in Westminster, many of them hearing a broadcast for the first time, were astonished.

The Wireless Officer interrupted the concert. 'Sir,' he said, 'the aircraft have just
taken off.' Within minutes they were in conversation with Lieutenant Newport, flying
at 8,000 feet, 20 miles away. After a friendly exchange with the Speaker of the House
of Commons, Newport sang a song. Seely then invited him and his pilot to dinner that
evening, and told them to bring along all pilots and observers flying within 20 miles
of them. Other voices came over the air, accepting the invitation.

Thus publicised, the IDE secured Treasury funding, and settled down to an ambitious programme of work, which, as Wallace describes it, 'embraced almost every branch of aviation except airframe and engine design'. The former WEE officers worked on Radio Direction Finding, the improvement of valves, deflection of wireless waves, and a system to help pilots land in fog. Meanwhile signals experts were brought in for 'long-range and ground-to-air visual signalling, signalling by invisible rays, navigation and recognition lights and audible sound signalling from aircraft.' Other aeronautical instruments were designed and tested — 'bomb-sights and gyro-stabilisers, sextants, drift-indicators, course-setting sights, pressure gauges, revolution and airspeed indicators, altimeters and flowmeters' — as well as 'safety belts, anti-glare goggles, oxygen supply systems, cockpit and clothing heating'. The IDE also applied high-speed cinematography for the first time to aeronautical research: film was shot at a rate of 450 frames per second and projected at 16, allowing the analysis of movements too small and too quick for the eye to register in real time. In this way 'the behaviour of aircraft on landing and taking off, the opening of parachutes, movement and vibration of propellers, and the atomisation of petrol jets in carburettors all became the concern of the photographic section.'[3]

In August 1920 a Handley Page 0/400 was loaded with instruments and used as a flying laboratory on a seven-day trip around the British Isles. On board were two pilots, a mechanic and four scientists who tried out different navigational aids along a 1140-mile route over a variety of landscapes and stretches of sea. Such experiments were to contribute valuably to the techniques of long-distance flying.

above
Senior staff at the Instrument Design Establishment, Biggin Hill, 1920. Roughly two thirds are civilians.

opposite
A Handley Page 0/400 bomber, painted by Stuart Reid. One of these aircraft was used as a flying laboratory for the Instrument Design Establishment at Biggin Hill on a trip around Britain in August 1920.

For landings in fog, the IDE set up three sound-detector stations around Biggin Hill to measure the height, speed and course of an approaching aircraft, which were relayed to the pilot by radio. At the northern end of the airfield a curved concrete disc 20 feet in diameter was installed, with a powerful klaxon at its focal point, which transmitted a carefully directed cone of sound into the air to a distance of 5,000 feet. An inbound pilot, unable to see the ground, could pick up the sound, then throttle back and glide in towards it, keeping to the centre of the beam until he touched down. The sound was extremely loud, with unfortunate side-effects – shattered windows, stampeding cattle — which made the experiments unpopular locally. The disc itself was also a physical hazard to flying. As things turned out it did not remain there long. In July 1923, as an economy measure, the Treasury decided that the IDE should be transferred to the Royal Aircraft Establishment at Farnborough.

Biggin Hill was now designated as a centre of anti-aircraft warfare, with the Army Anti-Aircraft School, a Night Flying Flight, a Home Defence squadron, and the Acoustical Section of the Royal Engineers stationed there. These four specialised groups, two from the Army, two from the Royal Air Force, would work together: the bombers of the Night Flight providing the live material on which the defenders, both ground and air, could practise and develop their defensive techniques. 'It will enable the problem of air defence to be studied, and personnel to be trained, on one of the aerodromes most essential to the aerial defence of London, almost inevitably the principal target of any aerial attack on Great Britain.'[4]

The use of sound to locate enemy guns had been developed by the Royal Artillery in the First World War. Microphones placed a certain distance apart would pick up the sound of a gun, and the strength and direction of the sound could be cross-referenced to fix its point of origin. A similar technique was now applied to detecting enemy aircraft, with a variety of receivers — cones mounted on rotating turrets, pits in the ground, curved concrete discs and walls — while operators wearing stethoscopes or headphones checked the strength and direction of the signal. The objective was to create an early warning system for air defence, crucial in any future war. Acoustic research continued at Biggin Hill into the mid 1930s, until the invention of radar suddenly made the sound-based systems redundant.[5] Although the technology was swiftly superseded, sound location continued to be used in combination with searchlights and anti-aircraft guns in the defence of Britain's cities during the Second World War.

In May 1923, 56 Squadron moved in to Biggin Hill with their Sopwith Snipes. For two months they provided the co-operation flying for the Army's anti-aircraft units, until the Night Flying Flight was formed on 1st July with three Vickers Vimy bombers and a Bristol Fighter. These were kept busy, flying by day for the Acoustical Section and by night for the AA School and the fighter squadron exercises. One fatal accident occurred, when a Vimy was used in shooting a war film during the winter of 1924 and a mock destruction of an aircraft turned into the real thing. Diving towards the snow-covered land trailing smoke as if he had been shot down, the pilot misjudged his height and crashed near Cudham, killing himself and his co-pilot, although the observer managed to jump out before impact and survived.

56 Squadron had served with distinction in the First World War and was regarded as one of the top squadrons in the Air Force. Based from 1920 to 1922 in Egypt, they moved to Biggin Hill in May 1923. In 1924 they converted from the Sopwith Snipe to the Gloster Grebe, their new machines painted with a red and white chequer pattern. A rising young officer of those years was William Dickson, who joined 56 at Biggin Hill as a Senior Flight Lieutenant in July 1926. Dickson had been one of the first naval pilots to make deck landings on ships during the First World War. He would go on to be Chief of the Air Staff, then Chief of the Defence Staff in the 1950s. In an interview recorded for the Imperial War Museum, he gave a vivid account of his time at Biggin Hill: 'Life at 56 Squadron was always full of incident and interest', he said. 'The year was taken up with local tactical training within the squadron, air firing practices to develop all the lessons of World War One, to make yourself efficient as a gunman, converging bombing, every sort of activity.'

Converging bombing was 'half tactic, half a sort of display item: three, five or sometimes seven aircraft all flying together, all dropping their bombs on a single target at the centre of the airfield or on an air bombing range. You would arrive in formation, break up, and then according to a drill which you had worked out in the hangar with chalk lines you would all come in in a certain pattern — carefully drilled, of course, any mistake and you would have collisions — you'd whirl away, round and round, each dropping his bombs, climbing up and resuming formation and flying away. It was very useful training, although perhaps you wouldn't have attacked a target in war exactly in that way, but the same idea was carried out in the next war.'

As for radio, he recalled that air-to-ground and ground-to-air communication were good, but air-to-air was not, particularly when the engine was working hard and the noise was great. For navigation, pilots were entirely dependent on map-reading; on exercises they repeated coming down out of the cloud and immediately being able to 'spot where you were and lead your squadron back to base'. They had no means of instrument flying in low visibility conditions.

Comparing Grebes and Siskins, Dickson thought them both good fighters, although the Siskin was more loosely braced, and during aerobatics 'you saw the wings bending and the wires moving about'. The Siskin was clearly a more demanding aeroplane, which pilots liked when they got used to it.

The squadron was often visited by the aircraft manufacturers, who 'had a great interest in the success of their products'. Their representatives would listen to the pilots' grumbles and 'put in little improvements all the time.'

Pilots were of three types: regular career officers from Cranwell who 'had pride and ambition in their hearts', short service officers who served for five or ten years, many

above
William Dickson (1898–1987), who flew with 56 Squadron at Biggin Hill in 1926–7. As temporary Station Commander he had to make the first jump when parachutes were introduced in 1927. He became Chief of the Air Staff in 1953.

opposite
The Gloster Grebe, the RAF's frontline fighter flown by 56 Squadron at Biggin Hill in 1923–7.

of them 'keen to show themselves as good as the Cranwell men', and sergeant pilots who were lower in rank and had to use a different Mess, but 'it made no difference, they were excellent pilots and they had the urge to get a commission.' The mixture of short service and other pilots 'worked splendidly. We were all bound together by a terrific enthusiasm for this new art: flying.' The whole station was a most exciting place to be, with 'young people in a state of discipline', their energy kept 'in the right direction'.

Very few of the officers were married, as there was no marriage allowance below the age of 30. Social life was 'what you would expect': rugby, squash, drinking beer and playing darts in local pubs. At formal guest nights in the Mess, people would 'get excited... with violent games after dinner in various physical ways', but no one was seriously affected by drink, which was 'highly disapproved of, as it would be letting the squadron down. It was all more or less under control.'

When the commanding officer fell ill in the winter of 1926-7, Dickson was put in charge. He was told one day that a Flight Lieutenant Grace had arrived from Henlow with a Vimy bomber to give pilots experience of the new Irvine parachute. It was 'all voluntary but highly recommended'. As acting CO, Dickson was expected to lead by example. He described what happened. 'It was mid-winter, a cold and frosty morning, very early so that it wouldn't interfere with flying the rest of the day... The Vimy was outside the hangars and I was the first volunteer. I climbed up onto a little platform at the base of the outer starboard strut, and a newly joined pilot officer who had also volunteered, Pilot Officer Pike, was on the outer port strut platform. (Pilot Officer Pike ultimately became Chief of the Air Staff, Sir Thomas Pike). The routine was we taxied out and the pilot, Grace, was at the controls, and you were stood on the little platform facing the rear, with your stomach up against the leading edge of the strut. And then the pilot would climb up to do his run up towards the centre of the airfield which was your dropping target, and when he approached it, at a very low altitude, say 1200 feet, he would give you a signal to shuffle your way round to the rear of the strut, hanging on tight with your left hand so that you didn't fall off before the parachute had opened. And you'd get in position, with your left hand on the strut and your right hand on the quick release, and you'd wait for the pilot's signal, and when he waved his arms you then, swallowing twice, would pull the ripcord. And whether you liked it or not suddenly there was a tremendous tug on your shoulders and you were pulled off. And of course that meant the parachute was open and you glided quickly down and hit the ground.'

A few of his companions let go of the strut but forgot to pull the ripcord. He thought they were 'goners' but they quickly remembered and opened their parachutes in time. All survived the exercise.

There was, however, one 'alarming incident'. A highly experienced parachutist, Corporal East, decided to break the record for a free-fall jump, using the 300-foot drop into Biggin Hill Valley for extra safety. 'The Vimy took off and we all watched. We saw East leave the Vimy — timed with a stopwatch — but there was drift and he fell on the road in front of the buses and was killed. It caused a terrific sensation, but it didn't put anyone off. It was just bad calculation and bad luck. Then we did several jumps from 6000 fee and that was that.'

'Subconsciously the knowledge you had the parachute gave you that extra confidence to do a little bit more with your aircraft. It was a breakthrough in morale.'[6]

Dickson's story illustrates some interesting points about the development of the Royal Air Force. New aeroplanes were brought in every three or four years, requiring constant learning. Life was disciplined and challenging, and morale was high. It is worth remembering, though, that in 1926 the RAF was only eight years old, with a very uncertain future. Its organisation, buildings, equipment, recruitment and training were based partly on Army and Navy examples, but much had been conceived from scratch. Lord Trenchard and a few capable assistants on his Air Staff had to think on a grand scale. They had to cost their ideas and bid for funding against sceptics in the Treasury and senior officers in the Army and Navy who believed that a separate Air Force was unnecessary.

One new aerodrome took four years to build and cost £750,000 — about the same price as a battle cruiser for the Navy. A fighter pilot took two years to train, an apprentice engine fitter three years. All needed instructors, accommodation, stores, money, transport, food, medical services, administrative support. A hint of what was involved in running an air force can be gathered from the following passage, about re-arming a squadron:

'[It is] not merely a matter of flying out the old aeroplanes and flying in the new ones. Before the new aeroplanes come in, you must re-man the flights with men who are qualified to service them and maintain them. The right number of tradesmen must be withdrawn from their posts scattered all over the service, anything up to a year ahead, and sent on courses within the service or at the makers' factories. These men would be the NCOs supervising the servicing crews on their new squadron, or station. The basic training courses for apprentices at Halton and at Cranwell would have to be rearranged two years or more ahead so that trainees could be directed in precisely the right numbers, allowing for training wastage (in other words, failures) into the right specialist streams and classes where they would be taught by properly qualified and trained instructors. The same would apply, over a shorter time scale, to the training of lower-skilled men at Manston, and to the provision of the right number of cooks and clerks. In a word, to ensure that a Battle squadron could be formed or armed in 1938 , the Manning Plan for 1934 would have to take account of it. Without computers.'

The list goes on…

'But the aeroplanes were not the only hardware to be supplied . The airframes and engines would not operate unless a whole world of spares were available in advance, all delivered and unpacked, and put away in the right order. Besides the actual spares, a variety of custom-built work benches and gigs and machine tools would have to be brought in and set up. Everything would have to be unpacked and checked and signed for, and sent back with complaints if it were not according to the specification. That meant a sea of paperwork, and though the apprentice clerks had been trained to deal with it, and the boy clerks before them, there were not enough of them. Nor were there ever enough typewriters, and photocopiers had not been invented . Everything in the end fell on the squadron commander.'[7]

In 1927, work was due to start on rebuilding and expanding Biggin Hill to form a permanent fighter station. The North Camp was still a series of wartime huts, the Officers' Mess was housed in a converted workshop, and more space was needed to accommodate aircraft with faster landing speeds. Cudham Lodge Farm was bought by the Air Ministry, its acres absorbed into the airfield, and the farmhouse — the scene of dinners and musical evenings for pilots in the First World War — demolished. The

The Officers' Mess at Biggin Hill, built 1929–32.

tenants of Forge Cottage and the Salt Box resisted offers to buy them out, and these businesses were still in private hands in 1939. (Forge Cottage and its tea-garden was destroyed by bombs in 1940; the Salt Box, which offered refreshments, petrol and automobile repairs, survived until 1954.)

A disagreement now arose between the Air Defence staff and the RAF Building Committee over where to locate the new Messes for Officers and NCOs. The decision to place them on the far (west) side of the main Westerham-Bromley road, out of the way of aircraft movements, was a compromise which worked well enough in peacetime but would prove difficult during the next war, when security became crucial. Construction eventually began in 1929, using standard designs, probably by the Scottish architect Archibald Bulloch, under the oversight of the Fine Arts Commission led by Sir Edwin Lutyens and Sir Reginald Blomfield: neo-classical red brick buildings ornamented with stone, housing the Officers' and NCOs' Messes, barrack-blocks, married quarters and offices. The style of the Officers' Mess was 'something between the country house and the large hotel'.[8] Rose beds and lawns were laid out around it, with tennis and squash courts in the grounds.

The building took three years, 1929–32. During this time, no fighter squadrons were in residence at Biggin Hill, but the work of the Anti-Aircraft School carried on, with help from the Night Flying Flight. In September 1932, two fighter squadrons, 23 and 32, moved in from nearby Kenley. Both squadrons were equipped at first with Bristol Bulldogs, although 23 had a Flight of Hawker Demons and soon converted to them entirely.

Lord Trenchard, remembered by history as the 'father of the Royal Air Force', had retired as Chief of the Air Staff in 1930. The leading figures in the service were now a group of men who had served under him, thoroughly understood his thinking, and planned for the future with a wide-ranging, practical, and scientifically informed intelligence that might stand for an ideal of public service in any age. These officers — Dowding, Harris, Tedder, Peck, Evill, Garrod and Edmonds — believed that sooner or later there was bound to be another war, which would be won or lost in the air. They set about preparing for this in 1931, with a plan that would permit Britain to face an enemy on equal terms by the spring of 1939. The basic elements of this plan — airfields, training, development of new aeroplanes and an early warning system — were in place by 1933. Biggin Hill's acoustic research experiments turned out not to be as useful as it had been hoped, but there was one more technical contribution which the staff were able to make, which played a crucial role in the Battle of Britain.

In August 1936 a three-day conference was held, on a secret topic. The participants were Squadron Leader RL Ragg (a navigation expert from Bomber Command), Dr B.G. Dickens (an Air Ministry scientist), Flight Lieutenant WPC Pretty (a Signals officer), Wing Commander EO Grenfell (the Station Commander), and the Chairman of the Aeronautical Research Committee, Henry Tizard.

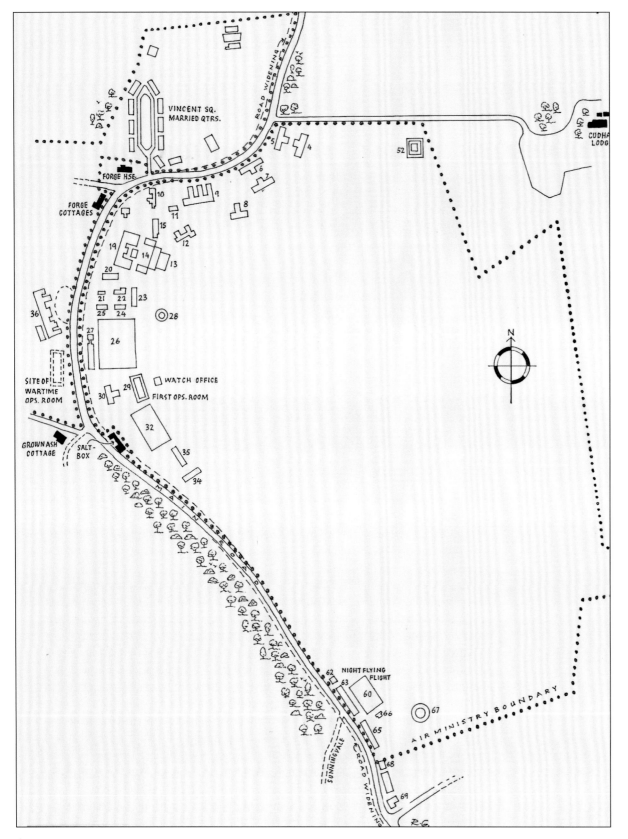

A plan of Biggin Hill in 1933

4 Barrack Block Design 'C'
5 Barrack Block Design 'C'
6 Barrack Block Design 'C'
7 Barrack Block Design 'C'
8 Sick Quarters
9 Combined Dining Room and Institute
10 Guard House Design 'C' (With Fire Party Access)
11 Ration Store
12 Sergeants' Mess
13 Fuel Store
14 MT Yard and Sheds
15 Airmen Pilots Quarters
19 Main Stores & Workshops
20 Armoury
21 Inflammable Store
22 Lubricant Store
23 Pilots Room, Locker Room, Airmen's Waiting Room
24 Parachute Store
25 Test House
26 Aeroplane Shed (Triple Bay)
27 Workshops
28 Compass Platform
29 Operations Block
30 Office Block (Stn HQ)
32 'F' Type Shed
34 MG Test Butt
35 W & B Yard (Without Section Office)
36 Officers' Mess & Quarters
52 Bulk Petrol Installation (Aviation)

Night Flying Section
60 Aeroplane Shed
62 Blacksmith's Shop
63 Woodwork Shop
65 Officers' Mess
66 Petrol Installation
67 Compass Platform
68 Battery House
69 Power House

Henry Tizard (1885–1959), chemist, inventor, and radar pioneer, Chairman of the Aeronautical Research Committee in 1936.

Tizard was the only man at the conference who knew its true purpose. His committee had encouraged — in great secrecy — the development of radar (or radio detection and ranging as it was originally called). By 1936 the potential of this technology was clear, but Tizard had a practical problem. Without giving away any technical details, he asked the participants how they would organise the interception of an approaching bomber force if 'by some means' they could have information about its height, bearing and distance, updated at one-minute intervals. The standard method of interception at that time was aircraft in flight patrolling the skies around Britain in the hope of spotting the enemy. This was both wasteful and ineffective. Ragg was asked to look into the navigation question, Pretty the communications, Dickens the wider scientific aspects. Three Hawker Harts were available to simulate the bomber force, while the Gloster Gauntlets of 32 Squadron went up as fighters.

The three specialists worked on the problem for five months, using the chart table in the Biggin Hill Operations Room and the manual instruments of the time: slide rule, protractor, ruler, dividers, pencil and paper. They were visited by senior officers and scientists, including one of the inventors of radar, Robert Watson-Watt, and the physicist Patrick Blackett, who were keen to know what progress they were making.

At last they cracked it. The solution turned out to be as simple as a school geometry lesson. The two flight-paths, bomber and fighter, could be drawn as two sides of

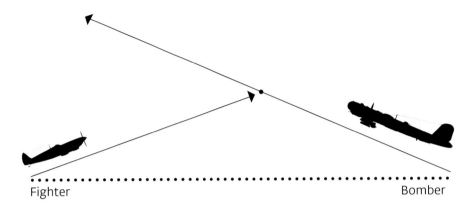

Fighter   Bomber

opposite
Gloster Gauntlets, flown by 32 Squadron
at Biggin Hill 1932–8.

next page
Logbook of Max Aitken, stationed at Biggin Hill with 601
Squadron in 1938.

an isosceles triangle (that is a triangle with two equal sides, forming equal angles with the base). The base of the triangle was a line drawn between the positions of the bomber and the fighter at any moment in time. If the fighter flew a course whose angle to the base line was the same as that of the bomber, their two paths would cross at the apex of the triangle. The fighter, being faster, would usually reach that point first, but could circle and wait. If the bomber should change course, the ground controller could quickly plot a new triangle and give a new heading to the fighter. The system was known as 'the Principle of Equal Angles'. Of 100 practice interceptions carried out in those months, 93 were successful. They tried it with untrained controllers, and it still worked.

What, though, was the 'some means' which produced the information that allowed this calculation to be made? It remained a secret until Ragg read a report in the press that the Germans knew of a British method of detecting aircraft with infra-red rays. He mentioned this to Tizard, who laughed and said, 'Good. Now I can tell you all about it!' The team were keen to conduct further experiments, but their job was done.

At Biggin Hill the Operations Room staff and 32 Squadron continued to practise interceptions. They received information from Bawdsey experimental radio-location station, tracking civil airliners en route from Europe to Croydon. The KLM morning flight from Amsterdam was a favourite. (Lufthansa flights, which were known to be manned by military pilots, were forbidden.) It was soon possible to guarantee interception of any airliner flying at altitudes between six and nine thousand feet, even in skies dense with cloud.

In 1936–7 the RAF reorganised itself into Fighter, Bomber, Coastal and Training Commands. Fighter Command was divided into four Groups, and each of the Groups into a number of Sectors, with a main fighter station and several satellite airfields. Biggin Hill was designated as the main station in C Sector of 11 Group, which stretched from Hastings to Sheerness (see map on pp. 56–7). The aerodrome was regularly photographed by Lufthansa crews as they flew to and from Croydon, and was marked as a key target for bombers in the coming conflict.

						TOTALS BROUGHT F
—	—	—	—	—		—
SEPTEMBER	16	DRAGONFLY	G.AEXN.	Self.	Bill Aitken.	Heston to Luton to see demonstr
"	16	"	G.AEXN.	Self.	"	Luton Heston {} new undercarri
"	22	DEMON	K.5716.	Self.		Night flying Sector reconn:
"	24	"	K.5721.	Self.		Sector reconnaissance
"	25	"	K.4527.	Self.	A/c Hardwick.	Sector map reading
		EUROPEAN SITUATION BECOMING ACUTE. HITLER STAKES HIS				
"	25	DRAGONFLY	G.AEXN.	Self.	Henry Cavendish	Hendon to Alan Butler's.
"	25.	"	G.AEXN.	Self.	"	Alan's back to Hendon.
"	26	MONDAY 6p.m. HAD DRINKS WITH PHILIP. SAM HOARE THE				
"	26	MONDAY 8.30p.m. HITLER SPEAKS IN BERLIN. REITERATES				
"	27.	SQUADRON CALLED UP FOR ACTIVE DUTY {Embo				
"	27.	DRAGONFLY	G.AEXN.	Self.		Hendon to Heston.
"	27.	SPEND DAY CAMOUFLAGING OUR MACHINES. FIRIN				
"	28.	GERMAN MOBILISATION ORDERED FOR 2.pr				
"	28	SQUADRON STANDING BY TO MOVE TO WAR STATION				
"	29	DEMON	K.4527.	Self.	Cpl Lamb.	Hendon to Biggin Hill.
"	29	"	K.5723.	Self.	A/c Vincent.	R/T. Exercise. Intercepti
"	29	"	K.5723.	Self.	A/c Vincent.	R/T. Exercise.
"	30	"	Y.N.A. K.5723.	Self.	A/c Warren.	Sector reconn: Wallon etc
"	30	"	Y.N.A.	Self.	A/c Warren	In search of Dope. Heston et

Summary for SEPTEMBER 1938		1. DEMON
Unit 601.F. SQDN Aircraft		2.
Date 30.9.38		3.
Signature F/Lt.		4. CIVIL FLYING

GRAND TOTAL [Cols. (1) to (10)]

702 Hrs. 45 Mins.

TOTALS CARRIED FOR

Au

SINGLE-ENGINE AIRCRAFT				MULTI-ENGINE AIRCRAFT						PASS-ENGER	INSTR./CLOUD FLYING [Incl. in cols. (1) to (10)]	
DAY		NIGHT		DAY			NIGHT					
	PILOT	DUAL	PILOT	DUAL	1st PILOT	2ND PILOT	DUAL	1st PILOT	2ND PILOT		DUAL	PILOT
	(2)	(3)	(4)	(5)	(6)	(7)	(8)	(9)	(10)	(11)	(12)	(13)

147·05

187·35

·20

·20

1·05

1·05 SQUADRON RE-OPENS AFTER SUMMER LEAVE.

·45

1·30

LAIMS ON THE CZECHS AND INSISTS ON THEM BEING MET.

ALAN SAYS HE DOES NOT BELIEVE THERE WILL BE WAR.

STATED BRITAIN HAD JUST GIVEN FRANCE EVERY ASSURANCE.

AIMS. WAR SEEMS PRETTY MUCH INEVITABLE.

4·30 A.M. VERY COLD AND RAINING.

·10

otice from Air Ministry. They are requisitioning G.AEW. So fly it to Heston. Last Flight?

UNS. CHANGING LOCKS ETC. 6·30 p.m. COCKTAIL PARTY

BRITISH FLEET MOBILISES

6 p.m. NEWS OF FOUR POWER CONFERENCE.

·15

SQUADRON AND ALL EQUIPMENT MOVE TO BIGGIN HILL.

·20

One slot stuck on landing through camouflage. Very bad swing on landing.

1·10

1·00

·35

6·40   1·05

1·30

+·50	477·45	·55	5 45		188·25			1·25	(10)	(11)	(12)	(13)
(1)	(2)	(3)	(4)	(5)	(6)	(7)	(8)	(9)				

+·50 477·45 55 1·45   189·75

1·25

above
Empire Air Day at Biggin Hill, 1937.

opposite
The Communications Room at Biggin Hill.
Watercolour by Elva Blacker.

While military preparations went on, the Royal Air Force mounted flying displays every summer to stimulate public support and attract young people to the service. Formation and aerobatic flying showed off the pilots' skills, while bombing attacks on dummy targets and anti-aircraft guns firing at drogues gave a taste of the sharp end of war. The Air Show at RAF Hendon was the greatest of these displays, but Biggin Hill ran its own Empire Air Days, which attracted crowds of 20,000 or more. In bright, sunny weather on 29th May 1937, 32 and 79 Squadrons raced each other for altitude, their Gloster Gauntlets visible from the ground as silvery splinters of light at 20,000 feet. A favourite attraction was the R/T demonstration where spectators paid sixpence to speak to a pilot flying at 5,000 feet and request a manoeuvre. The following year a Hurricane, protected by armed guards, stood on the airfield for the public to admire, and a Spitfire gave a dazzling aerial display, although the pilot had no time to land as he had five more shows to do that day.

When Britain declared war on Germany on 3rd September 1939, Biggin Hill was well prepared for the coming onslaught. Air raid shelters had been dug, buildings camouflaged, the staff thoroughly trained. The two resident squadrons (32 and 79) were equipped with Hurricanes in place of the old Gloster Gauntlets, and they had

recently been joined by 601, flying Blenheim light bombers. The airfield was defended by the 90th Anti-Aircraft Regiment and the Queen's Own Royal West Regiment. The Station Commander, 40-year-old Group Captain Richard Grice DFC, a veteran of the Royal Flying Corps, took the added precaution of arming 70 airmen with rifles — in case the Germans tried an airborne landing.

Pilot training included practice interceptions of enemy aircraft, exercises with local balloon and gun emplacements, formation flying, aerobatics, emergency scrambles, gunnery practice and set-piece fighter attacks. The set pieces turned out to be too formal for the lightning-fast unpredictability of real combat, as the First World War fighter pilots had discovered, but aerobatics were essential. As the Battle of Britain pilot Brian Kingcome explains: 'To be in aerial combat means you have to be prepared to fly in and out of all conceivable and inconceivable attitudes, angles and speeds, right way up and inverted, tightly in control and deliberately out of control. A pilot therefore has to know his aircraft's limits precisely — what it can and cannot do, its strengths and weaknesses, its virtues and mean streaks. The only way he can achieve this level of awareness is by constant experiment in the air, pushing a plane to its limits and checking its reaction to unnatural forces.'[9]

As well as the fighting men, the station's permanent staff consisted of:
- The Commanding Officer
- The Senior Controller, who communicated with the pilots by radio during missions
- Operations Room staff (mostly WAAFs, who began arriving in November 1939)
- The Intelligence Officer
- Secretaries, Typists and Telephonists
- Medical Officers, Orderlies and Nurses
- Cooks
- Mechanics and drivers for motor transport
- Firemen

Each squadron consisted of about 20 pilots and aircraft under
a Squadron Leader, plus
- Chief Administrative Officer (or Adjutant)
- an Intelligence Officer, who briefed pilots before missions and interviewed them on their return
- a Supplies Officer
- a Catering Officer
- a Medical Officer
- a Signals Officer
- an Armaments Officer
- an Engineering Officer
- 100 or more fitters, riggers, armourers and electricians who maintained and repaired the aeroplanes
- batmen, personal valets to the pilots ('the biggest boon to living and the most underrated of all forces personnel' according to Brian Kingcome. 'A batman was a confidant, friend and adviser, and there is no doubt that without him many a promising career would have come to a premature end.')

1 Wallace, RAF Biggin Hill, Chapter 5, p 59

2 Wallace's narrative includes this document:

Propositions put forward by the men of the W.E.E.

1. No man to be victimised.

2. Unless we receive a satisfactory answer from the Commandant we will put our case before Lord Weir, i.e. our deputation will proceed to his quarters.

(a) The men state that when they go sick the medical officer says that their complaints are due to the disgraceful conditions of the camp food and sanitary arrangements.

(b) Names of the men who can bear witness to the above statement can be supplied if necessary.

(c) We demand that Major XXXX shall be dismissed from this unit.

(d) Leave to be carried on in the normal way.

(e) The men demand that they leave the camp until it is put into a habitable condition by the civilian employees.

(f) Temporary release for those men who have jobs waiting and those who want to get jobs pending discharge. While the men are at home demobilisation must continue, and the men be advised by letter or telegram.

(g) Abolition of work on Saturday afternoons and Sundays.

(h) Restrictions placed on YMCA to be removed, prices in canteen to be lowered and a full explanation given as to what happens to PRI funds.

(i) Efficient transport to be provided for officers, NCOs and men.

3 Grievances.

Sanitary

a) Wash house – only five basins for 500 men.

b) Wet feet - no gum boots issued.

c) Dirty and leaking huts.

d) NO BATHS.

e) Inefficient latrines.

Food:

a) Shortage.

b) Badly cooked.

c) Dirty cookhouse staff.

d) Dining hall in a disgraceful condition.

e) Fully trained cooks should be substituted for present incompetent and inefficient youths.

These demands to be conceded by noon today.

3 Wallace, RAF Biggin Hill, 64

4 Minute from the Air Council to the Treasury, March 1922

5 The experiments, equipment and structures connected with this research are the subject of Peter Osborne's fascinating study, RAF Biggin Hill, The Other Side Of The Bump

6 Imperial War Museum: Dickson, William Forster (oral history) / IWM 3168

7 John James, The Paladins, 176–7

8 John James, The Paladins, 17

9 Kingcome, A Willingness to Die, 94

CHAPTER 3
THE SECOND WORLD WAR
1939–45

'I remember Biggin Hill with enormous affection. The strange double life, each one curiously detached from the other. One moment high above the earth, watching a sunrise not yet visible below, killing and and avoiding being killed; and the next chatting with the locals over a pint of beer in a cosy country pub as casually as though we had just stepped off the six o'clock from Waterloo after a day in the City.'
Brian Kingcome[1]

The first seven months of the Second World War, September 1939 to April 1940, were quiet in Britain. The Press had little to report on, and the period came to be known as 'the phoney war' or, as some wits had it, 'the bore war'. Dull as it may have seemed to many, however, vital preparations were being made. The building of ships, aeroplanes and vehicles, the manufacture of weapons and ammunition, the organisation of civil defence, the recruitment and training of servicemen — all had a chance to reach the levels that would be required in the approaching struggle.

The war began early at sea: shipping was attacked by U-boats, mines were laid by aircraft and surface raiders in the seas around Britain, while Royal Air Force fighter squadrons flew defensive patrols: the first 'kill' from Biggin Hill was a Dornier 17 shot down over Dover on 21st November 1939 by two Hurricanes of 79 Squadron.[2] The honours were shared by Flying Officer Jimmy Davies, an American, and Flight Sergeant Brown. Eight days later, 601 Squadron attacked a seaplane base at Borkum in the Friesian Islands, destroying five enemy aircraft and several boats.

In early December a harsh winter swept in, locking the airfield in snow and frost. Between January and March, the squadrons were moved to other airfields while deep air-raid shelters were dug and the first hard runway was completed.

In the Spring of 1940 the Nazi menace suddenly became real. German forces invaded Norway, Denmark, Belgium and Holland, and threatened an attack on France. French requests for help in the air were resisted by the Head of Britain's Fighter Command, Air Chief Marshal Sir Hugh Dowding, who wanted to keep a minimum of 52 squadrons in Britain for home defence. 79 Squadron, however, was sent to northern France to support the British Expeditionary Force while 610 Squadron took their place at Biggin Hill.

The German invasion of France in May 1940 was swift and pitiless. The French army, even with British support, was unable to prevent a rapid and humiliating defeat. 390,000 troops of the British Expeditionary Force were trapped near Dunkirk and from 26th May to 4th June a desperate attempt was made to evacuate them. This was 'Operation Dynamo'. Thanks to a brilliant co-ordinated effort of the Royal Navy and hundreds of private 'little ships', more than 338,000 men were brought safely back to England — the 'miracle of Dunkirk'.

While 32 and 79 Squadrons were away resting, and 610 was stationed at Gravesend, 213, 229 and 242 (Canadian) Squadrons operated from Biggin Hill and, with other squadrons in the south-east, did what they could to cover the retreat and protect the allied troops waiting on the beaches at Dunkirk. In nine days of fighting they shot down 36 German aircraft, plus 20 probables, for the loss of 14 Hurricanes and Spitfires. Much of the aerial combat occurred inland or several thousand feet above the pall of smoke that hung over Dunkirk; it was invisible to the men on the ground. This caused fierce resentment in the Army. One pilot, who baled out over the Channel, was shocked to be refused a lift home from a passing boat. The Prime Minister, Winston Churchill, felt it necessary to speak up for the RAF in Parliament: 'We must be careful not to assign to this deliverance the attributes of a victory. Wars are not won by evacuations. But there was a victory inside this deliverance, which should be noted. It was gained by the Royal Air Force.'

Whatever the bitterness over Dunkirk, it quickly gave way to feelings of gratitude as the front moved to the skies of southern England.

On 14th June 1940 the German army entered Paris. The whole of northern France was occupied, while the south formed a collaborationist government under Marshal Pétain with its capital at Vichy. The Germans now had control of an enormous arc of

previous page
Pilot Sergeant Douglas Corfe of 610 Squadron, stationed at Biggin Hill from May to August 1940. Corfe twice survived being shot down during the Battle of Britain. He died in combat over Malta in April 1942, aged 23.

left
The Withdrawal from Dunkirk, June 1940, painting by Charles Cundall.

right
Air Chief Marshal Sir Hugh Dowding, Head of Fighter Command during the Battle of Britain. This portrait, by the society photographer Carl Vandyk, dates from about 1930.

territory stretching from Norway to Brittany, with 400 airfields within striking distance of the British Isles. Hitler's plan was to force Britain to negotiate for peace. When this failed, he decided to invade, using the *Blitzkrieg* tactics that had worked so well up to now: terrorising the defenders with dive-bombing Stukas, seizing airfields with paratroops, and moving swiftly forward with armoured divisions on the ground. For this to succeed, an invasion fleet had to have an unopposed passage across the Channel, which would only be possible if the Luftwaffe dominated the skies. Hermann Göring, Supreme Commander of the Luftwaffe, promised a rapid destruction of the Royal Air Force and all British air defences.

Göring underestimated the fighting spirit of the RAF, its air defence system, and, as time went by, the British capacity for aircraft production. From July to October 1940 three thousand young airmen fought an epic battle which quickly became a legend, reminiscent of the defeat of the Spanish Armada and the Battle of Waterloo. Unlike those two great struggles, however, the Battle of Britain was fought in view of ordinary people, above gardens and farms, villages and towns.

'If we fail,' said Churchill in his most famous wartime speech, 'then the whole world, including the United States, including all that we have known and cared for, will sink into the abyss of a new Dark Age, made more sinister, and perhaps more protracted,

Genraloberst
Hans-Jürgen Stumpff

British and German
air forces
late July and August 1940

Royal Air Force (RAF)

 Fighter Command Group Headquarters (HQ)

 Group boundaries

 Sector boundaries

 Sector airfields

Luftwaffe (LW)

 Luftflotte Headquarters (HQ)

 Fliegerkorps and Fliegerdivision HQ

 Luftflotte boundaries

 Fliegerkorps boundaries

Luftwaffe Airfields

Selected LW units

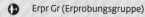 Erpr Gr (Erprobungsgruppe)

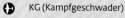 KG (Kampfgeschwader)

ZG (Zerstörergeschwader)

JG (Jagdgeschwader)

St G (Stukageschwader)

Air Vice-Marshal
Richard Saul

N

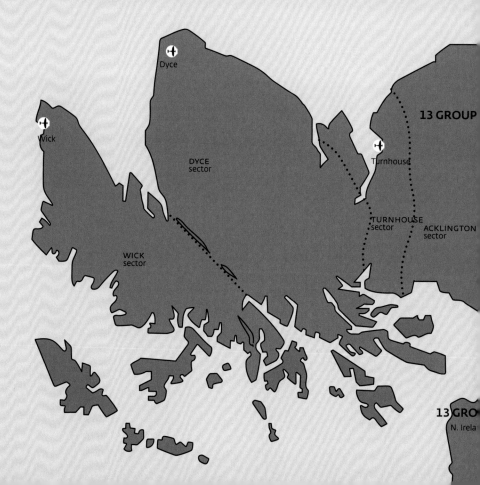

Dyce

Wick

13 GROUP

DYCE
sector

Turnhouse

TURNHOUSE
sector

ACKLINGTON
sector

WICK
sector

13 GRO

N. Irela

LUFTFLOTTE 2

LUFTFLOTTE 3

IX Fliegerdivision HQ
Soesterberg

Luftflotte 2 HQ
Brussels

IV FLIEGERKORPS
(rear HQ Compiègne)

II FLIEGERKORPS

Generalfeldmarschall
Albert Kesselring

Ghent
II Fliegerkorps HQ

Denain
Erpr Gr 210

Lille-Nord
KG 53

Arras
KG 2

Rosières-en-Santerre
KG 1

Luftflotte 3 HQ

Paris

Air Vice-Marshal
Trafford Leigh-Mallory

Montdidier
KG 1

Creil
KG 76

Deauville
V Fliegerdivision HQ

Generalfeldmarschall
Hugo Sperrle

St Omer
ZG 26

HQ Jafu 2
Wissant

Beauvais
I Fliegerkorps HQ

I FLIEGERKORPS

V FLIEGERKORPS

DEBDEN
sector

COLTISHALL
sector

HORNCHURCH
sector

11 GROUP

Le Havre
JG 2

Fliegerkorps
VIII Fliegerkorps HQ

NORTH
WEALD
sector

Watnall 12 HQ

Debden

N. Weald

BIGGIN HILL
sector

Biggin Hill

Duxford

KENLEY
sector

Caen
ST G 77

Hornchurch

Kenley

Digby

DUXFORD
sector

Wittering

Northolt

Air Vice-Marshal
Keith Park

Church
Fenton

Kirton-in-
Lindsay

Watnall 12 HQ

11 HQ
Uxbridge

Tangmere

Newcastle

3 HQ
sworth

Catterick

CHURCH
FENTON
sector

KIRTON-IN-
LINDSAY
sector

NORTHOLT
sector

TANGMERE
sector

HQ Jafu 3
Cherbourg

St Malo
ST G 2

CATTERICK
sector

12 GROUP

Middle Wallop

USWORTH
sector

WITTERING
sector

DIGBY
sector

MIDDLE WALLOP
sector

10 GROUP

Dinard

FILTON
sector

Channel Islands
(under German occupation)

PEMBREY
sector

Filton

Box
10 HQ

IV FLIEGERKORPS
(forward HQ Dinard)

ST EVAL
sector

Air Vice-Marshal
Sir Christopher Quintin Brand

St Eval

IX FLIEGERKORPS
(units in the field)

Brest
KG 40

0   50   100 km

25   50 miles

by the lights of perverted science.' Like Waterloo, the Battle of Britain was to be 'the nearest run thing you ever saw in your life'.[3]

The Biggin Hill Sector formed a crucial part of Fighter Command's 11 Group, defending London and the South-East. The Headquarters of 11 Group was at RAF Uxbridge, where reports from radar stations and the Observer Corps, filtered by Fighter Command at Bentley Priory, were received in the underground Operations Room. Groups of aircraft were represented by wooden blocks on a large plotting table, while 'tote boards' on the walls showed which squadrons were in action from which station. The commanders were able to see the 'big picture' and issue battle orders in time for the enemy to be intercepted before they reached their targets. The system allowed clear thinking at the strategic level, gave priorities and aims to Sector Controllers, and left the tactical initiative to squadron leaders and their men.

With three squadrons at Biggin Hill, each flying three to four times a day between July and October, the station saw the departure and return of over 1000 sorties during the battle. If we add the number of German raids on Biggin Hill, we see that in these short months alone the airfield was involved in around 1100 combat actions.

It all began quite peacefully. As Graham Wallace wrote in his book *RAF Biggin Hill*, 'In the warm, sun-bathed days of June 1940, it was a delightful station. Nestling among the green hills of Kent, slightly higher than most, Biggin Hill was proud that its work-shops, hangars, sick-bays and living-quarters — all the multifarious sections of an RAF station, including the gardens — were in perfect trim. The view across the valley from the terrace of the Officers' Mess remained as lovely as ever, an unfailing anodyne for ragged nerves.' [4]

This was all about to change.

Churchill made a stirring broadcast on the BBC on 18th June, and the Station Com-mander ordered copies of his speech to be pinned up for all to read. 'Let us therefore brace ourselves to our duties, and so bear ourselves that, if the British Empire and its Commonwealth last for a thousand years, men will still say, "This was their finest hour".'

On 25th June an engineer from de Havilland, Mr SC Bentley, arrived at Biggin Hill to convert the two-pitch propellers on the Spitfires and Hurricanes. These had required pilots to take off with the propeller in fine pitch, then switch to coarse pitch once airborne, and back to fine for landing. The need to switch manually had led to accidents.

War-time scenes at RAF Biggin Hill, painted by the artist Elva Blacker (1908–84), who served in the Women's Auxiliary Air Force as a driver in the Motor Transport Section from 1942 to 1944. Left: WAAF MT Rest Room (1944). Right: Conversation by a Window (undated).

above
Sir Winston Churchill, speaking to the nation from 10 Downing Street.

Mr Bentley, with the help of a Flight Sergeant and two fitters, worked through the night to convert the first operational Spitfire in the country to the constant-speed, variable-pitch propeller. Bentley spent the next week on the remaining fighters at the station. On his last day, dazed from lack of sleep, he walked into the wing of a stationary aircraft and knocked himself out.

On 27th June, the King visited Biggin Hill to hold an investiture and wish the squadrons good luck in the coming fight. Officers, airmen and WAAFS paraded for His Majesty, and a select group stood by to receive their medals. At the end one Distinguished Flying Cross remained unclaimed. It was intended for Jimmy Davies, the American pilot who had scored the first victory over the Luftwaffe in November. He had been shot down over France that morning, never to return.

The daily routine that summer was demanding in the extreme. Pilots, who slept in the Mess to the west of the airfield, were woken up at 3.45 each morning by their batmen with a cup of tea. (The batmen, of course, were up even earlier.) After washing and shaving (no beards were allowed, and it was a point of discipline to shave every day), they would dress, check their pockets were empty of items that might give useful information to the enemy, and go for breakfast in the mess (tea, toast, eggs and bacon). They were picked up and driven to their 'dispersals' — wooden huts at points around the airfield where their aeroplanes, parked overnight, were being checked and started up by the ground crews. Geoffrey Wellum describes the scene in his book *First Light*:

above
Sir Winston Churchill, speaking to the nation from 10 Downing Street.

right
Brian Kingcome (L) and Geoffrey Wellum (R), pilots of 92 Squadron based at Biggin Hill in 1940–1. Both survived the war and wrote vivid memoirs (*A Willingness to Die* and *First Light*).

Arrival at dispersal is for me always a moment. The drive round the perimeter track, masked headlights, the glow of somebody's cigarette and the squeal of brakes as the transport stops at the hut. No turning back now; committed. Here we go again.

I enter the hut and make for the flight board to check the 'Order of Battle'... I go to my locker and get my flying kit. It only seems ten minutes ago that we packed up for the day.

I remove my tie and open the collar of my shirt (far less sore on the back of the neck when you keep looking round). Now, where's my silk scarf? Don't say it's been lost. I take my parachute from the locker and, of course, my scarf is where I last threw it. I tie it round my neck, pick up my helmet and, slinging the chute over my shoulder, head for the door and the damp fresh early-morning air. Walk steadily towards my Spitfire, which is dispersed about fifty yards away. The sky is clear. In the slowly strengthening light the ghostly figures of the ground crews work methodically on the aircraft, removing covers and plugging in the starter trolleys....

It is first light and still rather beautiful; the birth of a new day. Reveries are suddenly and rudely broken. A raised voice comes from somewhere in the gloom, curt and to the point.

'OK. Clear? Contact.' ...

One after the other, Spitfires are starting up. The fitters warm up their engines. Twelve Merlins all at 1,200 revs or thereabouts. The power of the moment is

awe-inspiring. The still morning air reverberates with the sound of harnessed energy. Slipstreams flatten the grass behind the quivering aircraft. In its way it is exciting, wonderful and not without a certain beauty. It is also tragic; which of us is going to be killed this day?

Spitfires in 1940 carried 85 gallons of petrol, which gave them a range of 400 miles and about 100 minutes flying time, including 15 minutes combat at full throttle. Hurricanes were slower but had greater range (100 gallons/ 600 miles). The German fighters had similar capacities, but because they had to cross the Channel they had only about 20 minutes flying time over England.

Most RAF sorties during the Battle of Britain involved co-ordinated fighter attacks on large fleets of German bombers (Heinkel 111, Dornier 17, and Junkers 88) escorted by Messerschmitt 109 and 110 fighters. In the first phase of the battle, the Luftwaffe concentrated on disabling British radar stations and airfields in southern England. When the fighter defence proved tougher than expected they varied the routing and timing of the attacks, sending in waves at 20 or 30 minute intervals in order to catch RAF aircraft refuelling on the ground. The huge tonnage of explosives dropped on England also disrupted communications and electricity supplies, increasing the vulnerability of individual stations.

Biggin Hill squadrons flew almost every day that summer. Their pilots were turned into celebrities by the press. Thousands of stories were told — not just of shooting and being shot at, but also of mid-air collisions, jammed guns, cockpit and engine fires, emergency landings, blackouts in tight turns, baling out over land and sea, 'jumping' an unsuspecting enemy and being 'jumped' in turn, anxiously watching the fuel gauge and

Biggin Hill, August 1940. A Hurricane of 32 Squadron is refuelled while the pilot waits in the cockpit.

seeing the fate of others as their aircraft exploded or spun into the ground. There was good luck and bad, brilliant and not so brilliant flying, comedy, anguish, and countless acts of courage. The accounts by pilots themselves are varied and dramatic. This is Neville Duke's description of the day when he 'fired his guns at Jerry for the first time':

> We saw seven 109s, a few hundred feet below us, in pairs. I can still see them. They looked like a line of little rats, or mice, and when they saw us it was just as though they were bolting for their holes! They nosed straight over and into a vertical dive as we caught them up.
>
> Ronnie Fokes was in front, I was on his left and Roy Mottram was on his right, with the rest of the formation spread out behind — all of us leaving thick ropes of vapour trail behind. I picked a 109, and got astern and slightly to port just as he put his nose down to dive for home. I fired a short burst and was sure of a hit because a flash of flame came from his engine on the port side. But I was unable to follow down as another Spitfire came between us, and went down after him.
>
> Frankly I was terrifically excited and elated; and later on that evening, I jotted down my feelings in my diary. Here they are, for what they're worth:
>
> It is hard to remember your feelings and thoughts in a fight, especially your first. I don't think there is any feeling of fear, just an excited urge with a queer little feeling inside and the thought that you must get closer and closer. Knowing you have friends along with you helps more than anything else, I think. Perhaps your pulse beats faster. And it is a little harder to breathe; and although it is all over in a few seconds you feel very tired but with a queer feeling of elation inside you. This, I think, is because you know that the machine you have just fired at is your enemy and that he would shoot at you and kill you, if he could. I know I was not afraid, but very wary. After this squirt at the 109 I was chasing my own tail and my eyes were popping out of my head looking for other enemy aircraft. Where there were a dozen machines a few seconds ago, now there are none. Neither friend, nor foe. The sky seems empty. It's uncanny.[5]

Returning to base, they were welcomed by the Station Commander and the Intelligence Officer, whose job was to interview the pilots and record as clearly as possible what had happened in each encounter with the enemy. The pilots' accounts were personal impressions, snatched from the chaos of battle. They overlapped and sometimes contradicted each other. Both sides inevitably overestimated the number of 'kills'.

After a short rest while the aircraft was refuelled, rearmed, and checked for damage, the pilots could be back in the air again within 35 minutes. From dawn to dusk that summer they flew three or four sorties a day. They would read, sleep or play board games in between; an alternation of boredom and excitement.

'When we were stood down half an hour after dusk,' wrote Brian Kingcome, 'there was the choice of either scooting up to London, where ten shillings (the bulk of our day's pay of fourteen shillings) would cover an evening at Shepherd's and the Bag of Nails... or the White Hart at Brasted, where five shillings kept us in beer until the local bobby moved us on at closing time. Then, with a few girlfriends, on to our billets, a comfortable country house ... where one of our pilots, a pianist who could hold his own against any night club musician —and often did — would play into the small hours, and we would finally snatch an hour or two's sleep in arm chairs, fully dressed to save time and effort getting up for dawn readiness. Then to the dispersal hut with the unforgettable sound of Merlin engines warming up in the grey half-light.'[6]

After a few weeks of this intense frontline service, pilots were physically and mentally worn out, and were regularly withdrawn to quieter sectors for a rest. They observed in each other, but rarely in themselves, the signs of battle fatigue, nervous exhaustion and sometimes acute physical symptoms brought on by the punishing routine of broken sleep and the strain of mortal combat, alternating with evenings of beer, bonhomie and making light of the day's deadly business. They kept going, through comradeship, humour and an indomitable fighting spirit, but even the hardiest of them needed a break from time to time.

Johnny Kent, of 92 Squadron, wrote: 'Looking back on it now, and looking at photographs of myself taken about this time, there is no doubt that I had just about had it... I have no doubt now that, had I been allowed to continue, I would almost certainly have been killed as I know I was taking stupid and needless risks.'[7]

above
Pilots of 92 Squadron in their dispersal hut, Biggin Hill 1940.

opposite
Wing Commander Michael Crossley of 32 Squadron on a postwar visit to a favourite pub, the White Hart in Brasted. He is standing with the landlady, Kath Preston, by the blackout screen signed by pilots during the war.

next page
Documents in the National Archives relating to the bombing raid on 30th August 1940.

All the airfields of 11 Group were repeatedly attacked in the late summer of 1940. Biggin Hill was hardest hit in August, with raids on the 15th, 16th, 18th, and 30th — the last a particularly deadly bombardment. On that day ten German aircraft flew in at low-level carrying 1,000-pound bombs. Approaching along the Thames Estuary as if heading for London, they turned suddenly south, taking the defences by surprise. Biggin Hill's workshops, stores, barracks, meteorological office, transport yard, armoury, WAAF quarters and a hangar were destroyed. Thirty-nine people were killed and twenty-six injured.

Felicity Hanbury, in command of the station's WAAFs, described the day's events:

Our instructions were, once the station warning had been given, to go at the double into the nearest trench. I went. They were mainly officers in the trench.... I recollect particularly that Michael Crossley of 32 Squadron was also with us. I don't think I've ever felt so sorry for anyone. He had just landed his Hurricane for some repairs that had been needed and had been 'caught' on the ground. The trench rapidly filled and there we sat, packed like sardines, with tin hats on, waiting. One could hear the aircraft taking off — first one, then another, then another until all our Squadrons were airborne.

Then things happened quickly. Bombs fell at the far side of the aerodrome, each one seeming to come nearer until one fell just outside our trench. I remember thinking, 'I suppose one feels like this in an earthquake'. The vibration and blast were such that one felt that one's limbs must surely come apart. Bombs fell pretty

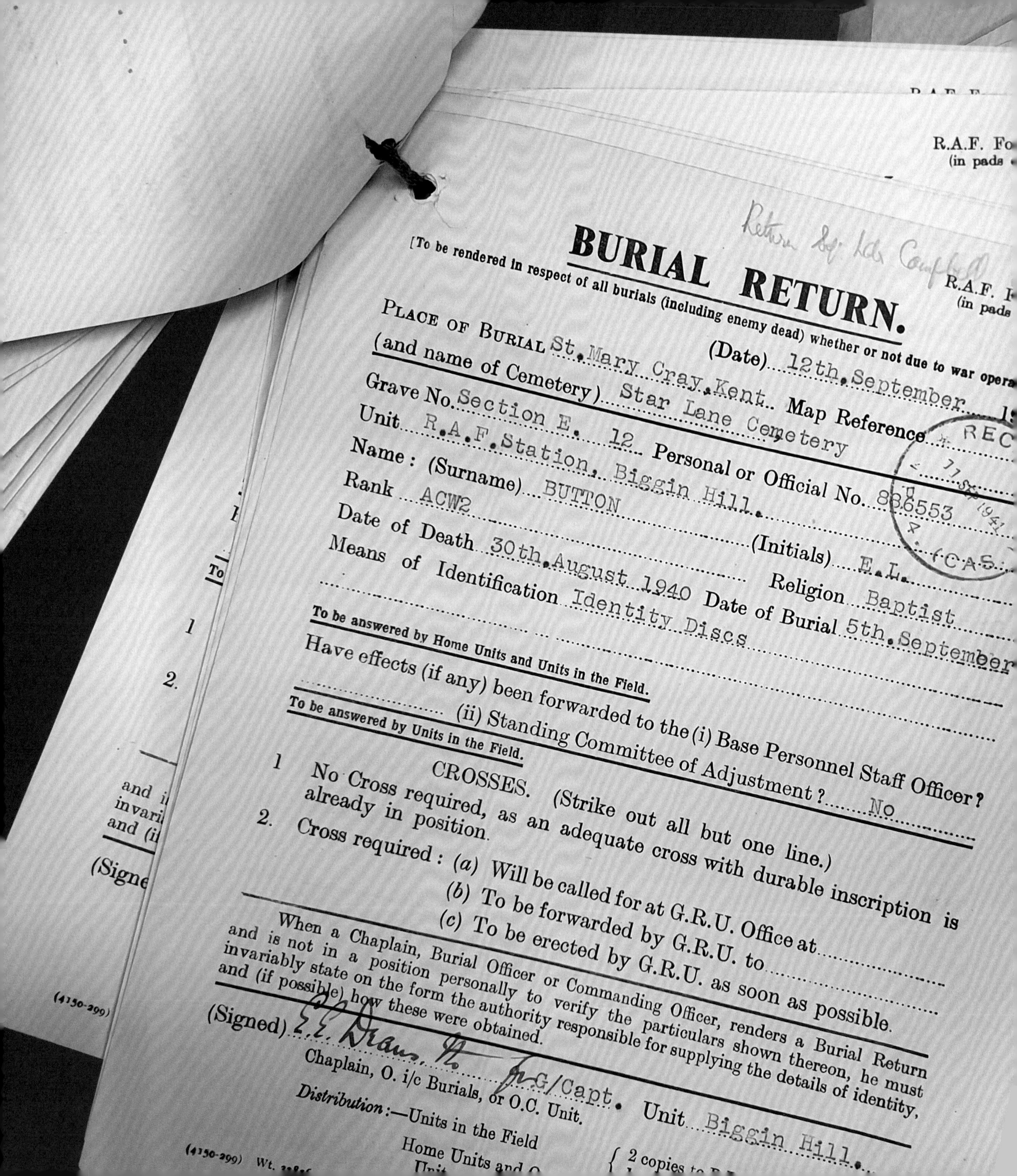

Return Sy Lds Complet...

R.A.F. Fo...
(in pads ...

R.A.F. ...
(in pads ...

BURIAL RETURN.

[To be rendered in respect of all burials (including enemy dead) whether or not due to war opera...

(Date) 12th September 1...

PLACE OF BURIAL St Mary Cray, Kent. Map Reference ...

(and name of Cemetery) Star Lane Cemetery

Grave No. Section E. 12. Personal or Official No. 886553

Unit R.A.F. Station, Biggin Hill.

Name: (Surname) BUTTON

Rank ACW2   (Initials) E.L.

Date of Death 30th August 1940   Religion Baptist

Means of Identification Identity Discs   Date of Burial 5th September

---

To be answered by Home Units and Units in the Field.

Have effects (if any) been forwarded to the (i) Base Personnel Staff Officer?

.... (ii) Standing Committee of Adjustment? No

---

To be answered by Units in the Field.

                CROSSES. (Strike out all but one line.)

1   No Cross required, as an adequate cross with durable inscription is already in position.

2   Cross required : (a) Will be called for at G.R.U. Office at ....

               (b) To be forwarded by G.R.U. to ....

               (c) To be erected by G.R.U. as soon as possible.

When a Chaplain, Burial Officer or Commanding Officer, renders a Burial Return, he must invariably state on the form the authority responsible for supplying the details of identity, and is not in a position personally to verify the particulars shown thereon, and (if possible) how these were obtained.

(Signed) E.E. Draw...   G/Capt.   Unit Biggin Hill.

Chaplain, O. i/c Burials, or O.C. Unit.

Distribution :—Units in the Field

Home Units and O...   { 2 copies to R...

(4150-299)

(4150-299) Wt. ...

AIR MINISTRY, (Dept...
LONDON, W.C.2.

(Dept. Q.J.)

30th November, 1940.

...as.

...dam,

I am directed to inform you that the Imperial
War Graves Commission is empowered to maintain service
war graves in this country.   No record is held in this
department of the place of burial of your son, the late
Aircraftman 2nd Class A. Hudson.   I am, therefore, to
request that you will be good enough to inform this
department of the name of the cemetery concerned and
the number of the grave, in order that his grave may
be registered with the Commission.

I am, Madam,
Your obedient...

for Director of...

Mrs. E.A.Hudson,
4, Brierly Street,
Warrington,
Lancs.

DOMINION OF NEW ZEALAND

Telephone : TEMPLE BAR 3611

....

OUR REF. **RAF. 1304/29/P3.**

YOUR REF.....................

HEADQUARTE...
ROYAL NEW ZE...
HALIFAX HOUSE,
LONDON, W.C.2.

22nd June, 19...

S.14 Cas.
Air Ministry.

Services.

for Airmen.

RAF. 886553. ACW.E.L. BUT...

It would be appreciated if your
would forward a copy of the report gi...
of the above named airwoman's death a...
her present burial location.

The cemetery at St Mary Cray, Orpington, with the graves of victims of the bombing raid of 30 August 1940.

continuously, the noise was indescribable, yet through it at intervals one could hear the splut-splut-splut of machine guns as plane after plane dived on its target.

Then there was a lull, broken only by the sounds of our aircraft returning to re-arm and re-fuel. A messenger arrived to say that one of the airmen's trenches on the edge of the aerodrome had been hit and would the Padre please come at once. I thought I had better go and see how the airwomen were getting on in their trenches. I climbed over the earth and rubble that had been blown into our trench and out into that lovely summer day. All was strangely quiet. The 'All-Clear' had not yet sounded. I made my way over mountains of hard chunky earth and round craters towards the WAAF Guard Room. As I approached there was a strong smell of gas; the mains had been hit. So had the airwomen's trench next to the WAAF Guard Room. As I went nearer I noticed a NAAFI girl lying by the side of the road. I went towards her and a voice from somewhere told me not to bother: she was dead. She was the first dead person I had ever seen. I remember thinking I must have a good look at her as I might have to get used to this kind of thing. I was relieved that my reactions were, at least, controllable.

When I arrived at the Guard Room, or what was left of it, there were many airmen already digging to reach the airwomen who had been trapped in their trench. The dry summer had made the ground unusually hard and their task was no light one. As the work went on, we must all have had the same thought: 'What shall we find when we reach them?' Ambulances and stretcher parties were standing by, a way was cleared and gradually, one by one, the airwomen were brought out. One was dead, several badly injured but, miraculously, the majority had escaped.

Flight Sergeant Gartside was brought out on a stretcher with, as was later discovered, a broken back. I took her hand and she smiled at me and said, 'Don't worry about me, Ma'am. I'm quite all right. Look after the others.' We found out later that she had countered any sign of panic, while they were waiting to be dug out, by her jokes and cheerfulness. She was afterwards awarded a Mention in Dispatches. When I had done all I could at the trench, seen people off to hospital, tucked others up in blankets and given them hot sweet tea, I made my way back towards Station Headquarters to discover how others had fared in their different sections. I noticed as I passed the NAAFI girl lying in the road that someone had put a blanket over her, covering her completely. Somehow this had a greater effect on me than when I had seen her the first time. It seemed so final, almost casual. I tried to put the picture out of my mind.[8]

She got to bed late that night and lay awake thinking of the day's events. One WAAF had been killed, a New Zealander named Edna Button, a 'smiling jolly girl who was loved by the airwomen'. Another, a driver called Lonsdale, had escaped death by a split second: 'She had just had time to jump out of her car and dive into a ditch when the siren sounded. The next moment she saw her car blown high into the air, to fall through the roof of one of the hangars.'[9]

By the next morning the telephone lines, gas and electricity supplies were restored, the bomb craters were filled in, and the fighters were flying again. This extraordinary feat was to be repeated several times: even when every hangar and office was in ruins, the station remained operational. Credit was given to the Commanding Officer, Richard Grice, for his leadership and determination, but he always thanked his staff on the base, as well as the civilian community, for their unfailing support.

Not everyone showed the Dunkirk spirit, however. Felicity Hanbury reports that when she walked round the village looking for emergency billets for girls bombed out of their accommodation, she was surprised by certain people's reactions: 'Some, on learning the purpose of our visit, rudely slammed their doors, while others made us stand on their doorstep and listen to their views on the RAF in general and Biggin Hill in particular. Had it not been for Biggin Hill the lives of innocent civilians would not have been in danger!... I was so tired that the attitude of these householders was almost more than I could bear, but I could not wait to argue with them; there were airwomen who had to be found beds before night.'[10]

As Felicity and a colleague were returning to the airfield, they heard sirens. They

Three WAAFs, Elizabeth Mortimer, Elspeth Henderson and Helen Turner, whose bravery on the evening of 31 August 1940 earned them the first Military Medals ever awarded to women.

quickly put on their tin hats and hurried towards a wood. A door opened in a nearby policeman's shelter and a voice called out, 'You'd better come in here.' Packed into the narrow space, almost suffocating in the heat, they heard the bombs falling with 'the same thunderous noises as the day before'.

When they emerged, they found the Station 'a sorry sight'. The Operations Room had taken a direct hit and the CO had been wounded in the eye by flying glass. Virtually all the remaining buildings, as well as the telephone and power lines, had been badly damaged. Ambulances and fire engines were arriving from Bromley and Westerham, but the road through the Station had been bombed and evacuation of casualties was difficult. Yet despite the physical violence, damage to morale was minimal. Like most air raids in history, this one merely hardened the resolve and anger of those on the receiving end.

That day three WAAFs — Elizabeth Mortimer, Helen Turner and Elspeth Henderson — showed such extraordinary courage that they were awarded Military Medals. Sergeant Elizabeth Mortimer was on the telephone switchboard at the Armoury, surrounded by high explosives. She continued working throughout the raid, relaying messages to the defence posts. When the all-clear sounded she ran round the airfield with a bundle of red flags, marking unexploded bombs. Returning pilots, seeing the flags, were able to avoid the UXBs and land safely.

Sergeant Helen Turner operated the switchboard next to the Operations Room. Ignoring orders to take shelter, she carried on working until a bomb fell outside and severed all her lines — except one. Corporal Elspeth Henderson, leading a team of plotters next door, kept talking to HQ at Uxbridge on the one remaining telephone line until she was knocked to the ground by the blast from the bomb that hit the Operations Room.

On Sunday 1st September a temporary Operations Room was set up in a local butcher's shop. Telephone and power lines were reconnected, and the dead were buried. The funeral service had scarcely begun when another German raid came in. Felicity Peake describes the scene:

It was another beautiful summer's day. The coffins had been laid beside a row of graves. No sooner had the Padre started to read the Burial Service than the civilian air raid warning sounded, followed almost immediately by the station sirens. Even the dead could not be buried in peace. The CO suggested to the civilian mourners that they would be well advised to take cover as best they could — the large gathering round the graves would have shown up as a considerable target. He gave his tin hat to one of the mourners and, taking mine, gave it to one of the others.

I shall never forget the expressions of sadness mingled with sudden uncertainty, bewilderment rather than fear, on the faces of those people. Many of them had travelled hundreds of miles to be present at the ceremony. One would have done anything at least to have spared them this and let them mourn their dead in peace. It was a heart-rending sight.

When the CO was satisfied that the mourners were well dispersed and as safe as they could be under the circumstances, he beckoned to me and we returned to the graveside to carry on with the Burial Service. We could not wait until the end of the raid. Many of the mourners had long journeys home. No one knew how long the raid would last. We returned to the first grave and stood to attention awaiting the continuation of the service but there was no sign of the Padre. To our dismay he was soon found taking cover in one of the graves. He was escorted away out of control. The CO summoned the Roman Catholic Padre, who was awaiting his turn, to continue the Service....

We could hear by now the all-too-familiar noise of enemy aircraft approaching, bombs dropping and dog fights: soon one could hear the zoom and roar of aircraft in combat immediately above us. I suppose one would not have been human if one had found it easy by that time to listen calmly to the Padre's words. As he read the Service he glanced up once or twice but nothing more than that. It took the utmost effort of willpower on my part not to look up. I also felt, acutely, the lack of my tin hat — it had become a very close friend — and an insane desire possessed me to put my hand on the top of my head for protection. The dog fight continued. The CO and I continued to stand to attention. It was in an agony of mind that I heard the well-known screech of a doomed aircraft as it dived, gathering speed, into the ground. Then the crash. Was it ours or theirs? Soon the all clear sounded, the mourners returned to the graveside and the service continued. [11]

Four days later, the CO flew a 'Maggie' (a Miles Magister, used as a communications aircraft) up to 10,000 feet to survey Biggin Hill from an enemy's point of view. Among the ruined buildings just one hangar appeared intact. He knew it was just a burnt-out shell, but it looked complete from above. Grice believed the Germans would continue to bomb the airfield until this hangar was destroyed, so he arranged to have it blown up by the Royal Engineers at precisely six p.m., when the bombers usually arrived. In fact no raid came that day, but the demolition went ahead — and the raids ceased. Whether this was the result of Grice's inspired act of destruction or because German air strategy switched, on September 7th, from attacking fighter stations to bombing London's docks, it is impossible to tell. Grice was censured by a Court of Enquiry for destroying Government property, but his staff at Biggin Hill supported him fully for preventing further loss of life, and he was awarded the OBE in 1941. [12]

Throughout the war, squadrons came and went, 52 of them in all. [13] The longest serving, 32 Squadron, was stationed at Biggin Hill for nine years. When they were transferred to Acklington in Northumberland on 25th August 1940, they were the top-scoring squadron in Fighter Command, with 102 enemy aircraft confirmed destroyed, one DSO and five DFCs. They had lost five pilots killed and one taken prisoner. As they departed, the squadron diary had this to say:

> Well, old Biggin Hill, 32 (F) Squadron bids you farewell. You brought us honour, excitement, fear, depression, happiness, tragedy, laughs, new associations, thrills — in short, every sentiment a man can experience in quick jumbled succession. Do we regret leaving you? Do the happiness and elation you brought us outweigh the sorrow and pain, and the indescribable 'eat, drink and be merry for tomorrow we die' sensation that each day brought? We don't know. We think perhaps not.
>
> No, we wouldn't have you again for worlds, but we wouldn't have missed you! You made men out of boys and we're grateful. So long, Biggin Hill. 32 Squadron will never forget you.

79 Squadron replaced 32 but only for two weeks, for they too had been serving in front-line stations for several months. On 7th September 1940, they were sent to Pembrey in Wales and their place was taken by 92 Squadron, who had a reputation for indiscipline — combined with a formidable combat record. Five of their officers wrote memoirs — Tony Bartley, Neville Duke, Johnny Kent, Brian Kingcome and Geoffrey Wellum. Two others had books written about them: Roger Bushell, mastermind of the 'Great Escape', and Robert Stanford Tuck, who had destroyed 27 enemy aircraft

Pilots of 32 Squadron in July 1940. Their commanding officer, Michael Crossley, stands third from right.

by the time he was shot down over France and captured in January 1942. The squadron attracted exceptional characters — men of rare talent like Bob Holland (a brilliant jazz pianist) or unusual size (like Tommy Thompson, who had been Public Schools Heavyweight Boxing Champion, and Johnny Bryson, 'a huge Canadian almost too big to fit into a Spitfire'). Brian Kingcome describes them as 'determined, committed young men, intent on squeezing the last drop of living from whatever life might be left to them', who also 'refused to take themselves or their existences too seriously.'[14]

When most of the buildings at Biggin Hill were flattened at the end of August 1940, the Station Commander decided that the pilots should be dispersed to private billets in the countryside. For the pilots of 92 Squadron a country house called Southwood was found. They ran it like a nightclub, with a resident jazz band and regular parties. Meanwhile the Station Headquarters, Operations Block, Transport, Equipment and WAAF Sections moved into requisitioned properties in Keston.

Three hundred airmen were billeted in the villages of Downe and Biggin Hill, while the majority (about a thousand) lived in the old barracks in the South Camp. Arthur Watts recalled: 'These quarters were 1914–18 vintage but, although old-fashioned, were comfortable and ideal from our point of view in that the cook house and canteen were in the same cavernous building. We enjoyed the comparative luxury of tumbling out of bed, straight into the next room for breakfast! For the next few weeks only the various squadrons' ground crew and other essential personnel occupied the airfield at night.'

Over the winter of 1940-41, the reconstruction of Biggin Hill began. Although the bombing raids had stopped, half-finished buildings, mud, and a working day that ended with black-out at 4.30 p.m. made life difficult for the administrative staff.

Their day started with a priority report to 11 Group Headquarters on the readiness-state of all aircraft; then the overnight signals had to be dealt with, the registered and secret mail; flying orders had to be dispatched to Biggin Hill's squadrons and those at West Malling, Gravesend and Hawkinge; then came Daily Routine Orders, Standing Orders, Courts of Inquiry, leave passes, ration books, petrol coupons and claims on the RAF and station benevolent funds. Any form of cohesion and discipline would have been impossible had it not been for the truly fantastic esprit de corps of the station.[15]

With the emergency over, the Station Commander ordered a return to normal routines and standards of smartness, with daily Physical Training at the hands of Sergeant 'Muscles' Freeman (Sports and Welfare Section), and airmen required to march correctly in parties when moving around the airfield. Pilots were forbidden to wear flying clothes in the Mess at night, and 92 Squadron were given a strict new Commanding Officer, Johnny Kent. A fearless Canadian who had previously served with a Polish squadron (303), Kent clashed with the men of 92. He was convinced that his fierce reprimands and insistence on the rules brought the squadron round to his way of thinking; they believed the opposite — that the CO gradually abandoned his officious attitude and came to see things their way. Kent gives one version in his memoirs, Brian Kingcome the other in his.[16] Whichever account is true, the Squadron and its CO soon gained each other's trust. Kent's courage and skill as a pilot, his leadership by example, played a decisive part.

In December 1940 Richard Grice reached the end of his two-year posting as Station Commander. He had guided the station through the preparations for war and its most testing days in the Battle of Britain. After complaining at his farewell party that the squadrons at Biggin Hill were 'the worst I ever knew, couldn't get them into the air; lazy lot of devils,' he was carried by six pilots shoulder-high through the Mess.

The new Station Commander was another Royal Flying Corps veteran, Group Captain F.O. Soden DFC, credited with 27 victories in the First World War and nicknamed 'Mongoose'. The name suited him: he was not afraid to take on big opponents. Shocked at the state of the buildings and the slow progress of reconstruction, he wrote to the Secretary of State for Air, 'I have just taken over here and the chaps are living under conditions of unnecessary filth and squalor: seldom, if ever, has so little been done for those few who have done so much for so many!' The Parliamentary Secretary to the Air Ministry was invited to visit, and was mildly offended by a notice pinned up in the Station Headquarters: 'Even more in this war than the last, have we to fight not with the enemy, but with the dull-witted at home.'[17]

Soden's outspoken remarks produced results. The rebuilding gathered pace. Even so, there was little to show for it by April: 'Poor old Biggin is in a pitiful state,' wrote Neville Duke, arriving there for the first time. 'Not a hangar standing, nearly all windows smashed, walls spattered and oceans of mud.'[18]

The weather was so foul in December 1940 that flying was possible on only 15 days, and morale was low. Christmas was celebrated in the traditional way, however, with the officers serving the airmen dinner, the bar open all day (and night), and a show by the forces' theatrical troupe, ENSA (Entertainments National Service Association). Someone found time to have Biggin Hill Christmas cards printed — a small but telling sign of unbroken resolve.

A good story is told by Graham Wallace about a late-night party that Christmas. A pretty WAAF, chatting to one of the older administrative officers, suddenly said, 'I'm tired. Let's go to bed.'

The officer had been hoping to suggest something of the kind himself, but had not yet plucked up the courage. All he could manage now was, 'Do you think we should?'

'Why not? It's my war work and, besides, you might be dead tomorrow.'

A young pilot officer overheard the conversation and told the girl that the only risk of death this man ran was suffocation amongst his files.

'Golly, his life must be dull!' she said. 'In that case, he'll need me all the more.'

On 25th November 1940, a new regime had come in at Fighter Command. Sir Hugh Dowding had been replaced as Commanding Officer by the more aggressively-minded Sholto Douglas, with Trafford Leigh-Mallory taking over from Keith Park at 11 Group. The role of the fighter squadrons now changed. Their main task was no longer the defence of the British Isles, but attacks on military targets in Europe. These were divided into five types, code-named Circus (a large fighter escort accompanying

above
Bob Stanford Tuck's Hurricane refuelling in the snow, January 1941 — a reminder that the war went on all year round. Although this picture was taken at RAF Coltishall, winter conditions at Biggin Hill were similarly harsh.

opposite
A Christmas card from the Canadian pilot Eric 'Timber' Woods, who was at Biggin Hill with 124 Squadron in the winter of 1941–2.

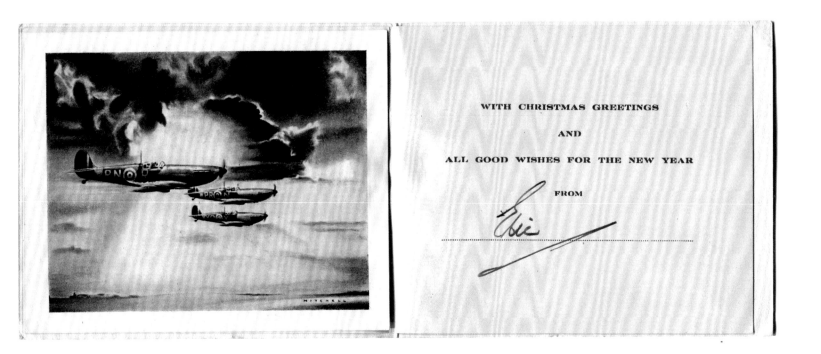

WITH CHRISTMAS GREETINGS

AND

ALL GOOD WISHES FOR THE NEW YEAR

FROM

bombers, designed to lure the Germans into the air), Ramrod (a bomber escort), Roadstead (attacks on enemy shipping), Rodeo (a sweep by fighters only), and Rhubarb (a low-level raid by a small group of fighters on enemy installations: trains, barges, lorries, bridges, etc). This new strategy exposed pilots to the same hazards that the Germans had faced in the Battle of Britain: flying over enemy territory with only 20 minutes' worth of fuel and the near-certainty of capture if one baled out or crash-landed. Losses were heavy and the strategy was controversial. On the positive side, it took the fight to the enemy, disrupted their lives, and, it was hoped, provided some cheer to the occupied populations of Europe.

Fighter squadrons were now grouped into a 'Wing' formation, each led by a Wing Commander. 'Sailor' Malan led the Biggin Hill Wing — consisting of 92, 609 and 74 Squadrons — while Douglas Bader commanded the Tangmere Wing.

By 1941 Biggin Hill was already a legend. 'Hardly a week passed,' writes Graham Wallace, 'without an official visit of some kind… The squadrons were besieged by journalists, photographers and script-writers who wanted to enjoy the war vicariously from a safe distance.' Reporters came from Australia, Canada, New Zealand, the West Indies, even from the Philippines. Archduke Felix of Austria arrived to collect stories for his American radio broadcasts, while the actor Leslie Howard gathered material about RJ Mitchell, designer of the Spitfire, for his film *The First of the Few*. Other stars — Noel Coward, Vivien Leigh, Laurence Olivier, Jack Warner, and the Gang Show — performed for the station personnel, as did the Windmill Theatre troupe with their

artistically posed nude tableaux. Winston Churchill too liked to drop in from time to time.[19]

A new CO, Group Captain Philip Barwell, arrived on 2nd June 1941. No less keen on discipline than his predecessors, Barwell was a popular figure, with the unusual habit of flying on squadron operations. This was officially discouraged, but he wanted to understand at first hand what his men were going through. He survived numerous sorties into France, but lost his life on the evening of 1st July 1942, shot down over the Channel by an inexperienced RAF pilot who mistook him for an enemy.[20]

Fighter squadrons came and went, some for a few weeks, others for months. As the air war shifted to the skies over Europe, Biggin Hill was no longer fighting for survival, yet its squadrons were in constant action, and led the field in the largest number of enemy aircraft destroyed.

By May 1943 the total was fast approaching 1,000. Excitement was mounting.

A raffle was started, with a prize of £150 for the winner and £300 for the lucky pilot. The press were primed and waiting. At 4.20 pm on 15th May, the Biggin Hill Wing, commanded by a 25 year-old New Zealander, Alan Deere, and consisting of 611 Squadron under the Canadian Jack Charles and the Free French 341 Squadron (Alsace) led by René Mouchotte, flew off to escort a bomber attack on Caen aerodrome. The total stood at 998, and the Operations Room was 'like a boxing arena with standing room only for the fans'.[21] Over the radio came the voice of the Wing Leader, Alan Deere, code-name Brutus: 'Brutus aircraft, look out! Bandits climbing at three o'clock.'

A pack of Focke-Wulf 190s had taken off to intercept the raid. 611 Squadron dived down into the attack, with 341 giving cover from above. Jack Charles destroyed one

left
A line of pilot officers cheering King George VI on 27 June 1940. The central three were key figures at Biggin Hill. Left to right: JL Allen, RR Stanford Tuck, AC. Deere, AG 'Sailor' Malan, JA Leathart.

right
Group Captain Philip 'Dickie' Barwell, Commanding Officer at Biggin Hill from June 1941 to July 1942. He is seen here shaking hands with the Duke of Kent.

left
New Zealander Alan Deere, one of several fighter aces who wrote war memoirs. Deere led the sortie to France which resulted in the destruction of the 1000th enemy aircraft by fighters based at Biggin Hill.

right
Jack Charles (Canada) and René Mouchotte (France) share the honours for shooting down the 1000th enemy aircraft.

German fighter, then, turning and climbing steeply, took down another. At the same time, 3,000 feet above, René Mouchotte spotted a 190 under his starboard wing, followed it round and fired from dead astern. The Focke-Wulf disintegrated. Suddenly the total was 1001.

Who had got the 1,000th? When the Wing returned to Biggin Hill, Mouchotte and Charles each modestly gave credit to the other. The Station Commander, 'Sailor' Malan, who had flown on the mission, decided they should share the honour and the prize.

Al Deere remarked on the international nature of the battle. 'Thus it came about that the 1,000th enemy aircraft destroyed by pilots operating from Biggin Hill was shared by a Canadian and a Frenchman while a South African Station Commander and a New Zealand Wing Leader looked on.' [22]

The event was celebrated with a dinner-dance at the Grosvenor House Hotel in London. A thousand guests were invited, including the heads of Fighter and Bomber Command and all the pilots of 11 Group who could be spared from duty that night. The sumptuous banquet featured three large lobsters — labelled 'Hitler', 'Goebbels' and 'Mussolini'. Three RAF bands played, drinks were free, and the Windmill Theatre laid on a special cabaret. As the party ended, a fleet of London taxis offered free rides home to Biggin Hill. 'Sailor' Malan, who celebrated the birth of his second child that night, returned the favour with a dinner later that year for fifty London cabbies as guests of honour in the Officers' Mess at Biggin Hill. [23]

A celebration of a different kind was proposed by the station's chaplain, Squadron Leader Cecil King. He felt that a tribute should be paid to the pilots from Biggin Hill who had lost their lives. A disused army hut was consecrated as St George's

Chapel of Remembrance, with an oak reredos recording the names of the fallen and the names of the great engagements: Dunkirk, the Battle of Britain, Dieppe. The Memorial was dedicated on 19th September, and the reredos unveiled by the Station Commander, 'Sailor' Malan.

Although the chapel was destroyed by fire after the war, it was replaced by a new brick building opened by Sir Hugh Dowding in 1951. The reredos was saved and now bears 454 names.[24]

Later in the war, as allied troops landed in Italy (1943) and France (1944), and the RAF concentrated more and more on bombing Germany, Biggin Hill's military importance faded. Yet its fame remained, and even grew. A symbol of Britain's fighting spirit, the station had welcomed numerous overseas pilots, sometimes entire squadrons of them. From Poland, Czechoslovakia, Belgium, Norway, France and Holland came a series of determined, resourceful characters who had escaped the Germans along clandestine routes. Americans arrived too, flying as volunteers well before their nation entered the war, while several girls with private pilot's licences joined the Air Transport Auxiliary and ferried aircraft between airfields, factories and workshops. From Canada, South Africa, India, Australia and New Zealand came men from the imperial air forces; among them Johnny Checketts, Alan Deere, Johnny Kent and Adolph 'Sailor' Malan, Station Commander at Biggin Hill from January to October 1943, a crack shot whose ten rules of air fighting were pinned up on notice boards at RAF Stations around the country.

Among those who left their mark and carried the name of Biggin Hill around the world were:

TEN of MY RULES
for AIR FIGHTING.

1 *Wait until you see the whites of his eyes.* Fire short bursts of 1 to 2 seconds and only when your sights are definitely 'ON'.

2 Whilst shooting think of nothing else, brace the whole of the body; have both hands on the stick, concentrate on your ring sight.

3 Always keep a sharp lookout. "Keep your finger out"!

4 Height gives You the initiative.

5 Always turn and face the attack.

6 Make your decisions promptly. It is better to act quickly even though your tactics are not the best.

7 Never fly straight and level for more than 30 seconds in the combat area.

8 When diving to attack always leave a proportion of your formation above to act as top guard.

9 INITIATIVE, AGGRESSION, AIR DISCIPLINE, and TEAM WORK are words that MEAN something in Air Fighting.

10 Go in quickly – Punch hard – Get out!

above left
'Sailor' Malan's ten rules for air fighting. These rules were posted on fighter station notice boards around the country. Malan was one of the top-scoring aces of the war. He was Officer Commanding RAF Biggin Hill from January to October 1943.

above right
19th August 1942. Pilots of 401 Squadron (Royal Canadian Air Force) in front of a Spitfire Mark IX. No 401 was at Biggin Hill in August and September 1942 and again from October 1943 to April 1944.

• Polish Air Force officers who served in 32 Squadron, based at Biggin Hill from May to August 1940. Boleslaw Wasnowalski (1916–1940) and Karol Pniak (1910–1980) were two of the 145 fighter pilots from the Polish Air Force who fought in the Battle of Britain. Between them 'Vodka' and 'Cognac' shot down 12 enemy aircraft. Having to learn a new language and culture, grappling with unfamiliar controls and flying disciplines, using imperial not metric measurements, and often posted in ones and twos to British squadrons, the Poles' achievements are all the more remarkable.[25]

• The Belgian pilots of 609 Squadron, famed for their dashing style and colourful radio French, were stationed at Biggin Hill in the summer of 1941; these included Jean Offenberg (the first Belgian to receive the Distinguished Flying Cross), Roger Malengrau (whose Spitfire engine was knocked out by cannon fire over Gravelines, yet managed a record-breaking 20-mile glide across the sea to Kent), Comte Rodolphe de Hemricourt de Grunne, who had flown with 32 Squadron during the Battle of Britain but drowned in the English Channel after baling out of his Spitfire in May 1941; and Vicky Ortmans, a serial survivor who was shot down and baled out no less than five times (he was taken prisoner after the fifth).

• The Royal Canadian Air Force Squadrons (401, 411 and 412, from 13th October 1943 to 15th April 1944), flew Spitfires in support of huge fleets of American heavy bombers on raids into Germany. Flight Lieutenant 'Screwball' Beurling of 412 Squadron was one of the top-scoring aces of the war, with 31 kills.

• The Eagle Squadrons (133, 222 and 602), made up of US volunteers were stationed at Biggin Hill from 3rd May to 28th September 1942. Their commanders were 'Cobey' King, a former Hollywood stunt pilot, and 'Red' McColpin, renowned for his brilliance at poker, who was the first of the Americans to destroy an enemy fighter. They were

joined in August 1942 by a regular American unit, the 307th Pursuit. Although the Eagle Squadrons stayed only a few months at Biggin Hill, their pilots had time to adopt a local pub, The Queen's Head at Downe, where they were photographed playing darts and shove ha'penny, and left many happy memories. As their time at Biggin Hill drew to an end, disaster struck one of these Eagle Squadrons: detailed to escort a Flying Fortress raid on the French port of Brest on 26th September 1942, 133 Squadron were caught by 100 mph winds which blew them far to the south of their target. By the time they turned for home, their fuel was running out. Eleven of them were forced to land in France, where they were captured. The twelfth crashed into the cliffs of the Lizard peninsula as he tried to glide home. Two days later, as the Eagle Squadrons formally joined their own Air Force in a ceremony at Debden, Air Marshal Sholto Douglas declared, 'We of Fighter Command deeply regret this parting, for in the course of the past eighteen months we have seen the stuff of which you are made, and we could not ask for better companions with which to see the fight through to the finish.'

• 485 Squadron of the Royal New Zealand Air Force, led by Johnny Checketts (1st July to 18th October 1943).

• Two Free French Squadrons: Île de France (340) and Alsace (341). There were some remarkable characters among them. Three of them feature in Alan Deere's memoir, *Nine Lives*:

'Tall and thin, [René Mouchotte, the Commandant of 341] was always immaculately dressed and very rarely to be seen without a long stylish cigarette holder held either between delicate fingers or gently gripping teeth. But René's appearance belied his true worth as a leader and a fighter pilot. He was dedicated to the liberation of his country and to him there was no joy in life so long as the Boche (he had a singularly expressive way of pronouncing the word) was on French soil. A quiet and reserved

officer on the ground; an aggressive and purposeful fighter in the air. Supporting René were his two flight commanders, Captains Martell and Boudier, the former a gentle giant of sixteen and a half stone, but a killer in action, and the latter a small quiet man who was never over-excited, an ideal trait among naturally excitable Frenchmen'.

René Mouchotte, described by one of his pilots as 'the kind of man for whom you would get yourself killed without discussion, almost with pleasure', died in battle over St Omer on 27th August 1943.

Pierre Clostermann, who wrote these words about Mouchotte, was to provide the only eye-witness account by a foreigner of Biggin Hill at war. His book, *Le Grand Cirque (The Big Show)*, is a masterpiece among war memoirs. It includes a gripping account of his first sortie, beginning with a long morning's wait in the dispersal hut, playing Monopoly and listening to old favourites on the gramophone, while two comrades tinker with a motorcycle outside the window.

The telephone rings, and everyone looks up with tense faces.

'Early lunch for pilots. There's a show on!' shouts the orderly.

Commandant Mouchotte arrives and the men gather round a board 'studded with twelve nails on which would shortly hang 12 metal Spitfire silhouettes, each bearing a name.' Here the Squadron's order of battle is displayed. Those not chosen to fly 'mutter restlessly among themselves'.

The mess truck arrives and they go to lunch — soup, sausages and mash — but Clostermann is too nervous to eat. He is wondering how he will react in battle, and tries to guess what is going on in the mind of a seasoned Canadian pilot from 611 Squadron 'calmly asking the WAAF waitress for a second helping of mashed potatoes'. Other pilots are discussing football.

At 1230 they are called to the briefing:

> We moved in small silent groups towards the Intelligence Room. First, a room cluttered up with photos, maps, easy chairs, technical papers and confidential Air Ministry publications. In a corner a small low door gave access to the briefing room down a few steps. The atmosphere caught you by the throat the moment you put your foot inside the door. The first thing you saw was the big map of our sector of operations, completely covering the wall behind the platform; South-East England, London, the Thames, the Channel, the North Sea, Holland, Belgium, and France as far west as Cherbourg. On the map a red ribbon joined Biggin Hill to Amiens, turned back through Saint-Pol, and returned via Boulogne to Dungeness — our route for the day's sortie.
>
> The pilots pushed in and found themselves somewhere to sit, amid the muffled stamping of flying boots and the scratching of matches. Smoke began to curl up from cigarettes held in nervous fingers. From the ceiling hung models of Allied and German aircraft. On the walls were pinned photos of Focke-Wulfs and Messerschmitt 109s taken from every angle, with diagrams giving the corresponding aiming deflections. The vital battle slogans were posted everywhere...
>
> 'The Hun is always in the sun.'
> 'Never go after a Jerry you have hit. Another will get you for certain.'
> 'Silence on the radio. Don't jam your RT channel!'
> 'If you are brought down over enemy territory, escape. If you are caught, keep your trap shut...'
>
> The navy-blue French uniforms stood out among the blue-grey battle dress of the British and Canadians, but the same hearts beat beneath them all. A sound of brakes was heard outside. Doors banged. Everyone got up noisily. Group Captain Malan, DSO DFC, and Wing Commanders Al Deere and De La Torre came in, followed by Mouchotte and Jack Charles, OC 485 Squadron. Malan leaned against the wall in a corner, De La Torre and Al Deere went up on the platform.

Pierre Clostermann, a Free French pilot of 341 (Alsace) Squadron, author of the war memoir *Le Grand Cirque* (*The Big Show*). No 341 was at Biggin Hill from March to October 1943.

'Sit down, chaps,' said De La Torre. Silence . He started to read Form D in his monotonous voice:

'This afternoon the Wing is taking part in Circus No. 87. H hour is 1325 hours. Seventy-two Flying Fortresses will bomb Amiens Glissy airfield. Close escort will be provided at 16000 ft, by seven Wings, i.e. 14 squadrons of Spitfire Vs...'

Detailed instructions follow, including the expected fighter response from the Luftwaffe, radio frequencies, call signs, compass bearings and timings. The pilots scribble notes on the backs of their hands.

Then a rush for the door and the wagons.

The weather was superb and for three days the sun had been unusually bright for the time of year. At the dispersal everyone made a beeline for his locker. I carefully emptied my pockets — no revealing bus tickets must be left, no addressed envelopes which might give away my airfield to the Hun. I took off my collar and tie and put on a silk scarf instead. I drew the thick white regulation pullover over a sheepskin waistcoat. I pulled on over my socks thick woollen stockings up to my thighs. Then on top of those my fleece lined boots, tucking in my trousers. I slipped my hunting knife into the left boot, my maps into the right. I loaded my Smith and Wesson service revolver and passed the lanyard round my neck. In the pockets of my Mae West were my 'escape kit' and my emergency rations.

My fitter came for my parachute and dinghy, to place them in the seat of the aircraft, together with my helmet, whose earphones and mask the electrician would connect to the radio and the oxygen bottles.

By 1315 he had been strapped in to his Spitfire, tested the radio, sight and gun camera, armed the guns and adjusted the rear vision mirror.

People were busy all round the field. In the distance Deere's car stopped by his aircraft under the control tower. He was wearing a white flying suit and he slipped quickly into his cockpit. The fire crew took up their positions on the running boards of the tender and the medical orderlies in the ambulance. The hour was approaching.

1319 hours. Deep silence over the airfield. Not a movement anywhere. The pilots had their eyes glued on Mouchotte who was consulting his watch. By each aircraft a fitter stood motionless, his finger on the switch of the auxiliary starter batteries. Another stood guard by the fire extinguishers lying on the grass at the ready. My parachute buckle was badly placed and was torturing me, but it was too late to adjust it.

At 1320 Mouchotte glanced round the twelve Spitfires, then began to manipulate his pumps. A rasping rattle from the starter, then his propeller began to turn. Feverishly I switched on.

'All clear? — switches ON!'

Kept in perfect trim, my Rolls-Royce engine started first shot. The fitters rushed round, removing chocks, dragging batteries away, hanging onto the wing tips to help the aircraft pivot. Mouchotte's NL-L was already taxiing to the northern end of the field.

1322 hours. The engines of 611 were turning and the 12 Spitfires beginning to line up on either side of Deere's in a cloud of dust. We lined up behind them in combat formation. I took up my position, my wingtip almost touching Martell's. I was sweating.

1324 hours. The 26 aircraft were all ready, their engines ticking over, wings glinting in the sun. The pilots adjusted their goggles and adjusted their harness.

1325 hours. A white rocket rose from the control tower. Deere raised his arm and the 13 aircraft of 611 squadron started forward. In his turn Mouchotte raised his gloved hand and slowly opened the throttle. Eyes fixed on Martell's wingtip, and my hands moist, I followed. The tails went up, the Spitfires began to bounce clumsily on their narrow undercarriages, the wheels left the ground — we were airborne.

Armourers, riggers and fitters

'A squadron in war is a sensitive body. The men who fly find glory and die young. The men on the ground live long with little acclaim but their work is endlessly exacting, and if they fumble once a pilot is likely to die.'

Paul Brickhill, *Reach for the Sky*

left
Press photograph released in January 1943 with the headline 'Britain's Ace Fighter Pilot Takes Command of a Crack Fighter Station'.
Left to right: Squadron Leader de la Torre (Station Intelligence Officer), Group Captain AG 'Sailor' Malan (Station Commander), Wing Commander RM Milne (Wing Leader), Squadron Leader WAK Igoe (Fighter Controller).

opposite
An armourer re-arming a Spitfire, Biggin Hill, September 1940

Fighter pilots were popular heroes. Many wrote books about their experiences, or had books written about them. *First Light, Reach for the Sky, The Last Enemy, Wing Leader* — these have become classics of war literature. They make thrilling reading, and not just for schoolboys: vivid, thoughtful accounts by brave young men who made light of their encounters with death, yet lived every moment with extraordinary intensity.

All mention the ground staff, especially station commanders, controllers and intelligence officers, whom they spoke to every day. These were older men, aged 35 or more, many of them veterans of the Royal Flying Corps. Their presence — kindly, watchful and stern, rather like old-fashioned schoolmasters — was taken for granted until one of them was posted elsewhere, or died, and suddenly the loss was felt.

Alan Deere writes with special fondness of the Senior Controller, Bill Igoe:

Bill had been in the RAF before the war as a fighter pilot but had been invalided out as a result of a serious flying accident, and had become a most successful businessman in the City. He rejoined the day the war broke out and got himself on to controlling as the next best thing to flying, for which he was rejected. With a background of fairly recent flying experience Bill appreciated more than any other controller I knew the sort of information pilots required passed to them in the air and he had the personality and ability to put it over. What a bundle of Irish energy he was — whether it was on the squash court or rugger field, and he was damn good at both games — and the operation room always took on a new lease of life when he appeared.[26]

The pilots also paid tribute to the men who kept the aircraft in working order. Each had his dedicated team of three: the rigger for the airframe, the fitter for the engine and propeller, and the armourer who cleaned and loaded the guns. Squadrons also had their specialists in radio, electrics and instruments. For every pilot, therefore, at least five support crew were needed. 'Theirs was not an exciting or highly rewarding war,' wrote one pilot; 'just one of graft and dogged hard work all hours of the day and night. The salt of the earth, without a doubt. More than that, supportive friends, who took as much interest in my welfare as I did myself and were as proud of my success as if it were their own.'[27]

Essential as they were, these men have slipped into the shadows. We know few of their names and little of their lives. The Imperial War Museum holds some recordings of interviews, and one or two books and specialist websites give useful information, but ground crews did not write their memoirs, nor did they have the duels with death that made such exciting stories. The slang name for them — 'erks', probably derived from 'aircs' (aircraftmen) — is an unglamorous word that reflects their humble role.

The historian Joshua Levine collected a number of testimonies in his book *Forgotten Voices of the Blitz and the Battle for Britain*. Among them are these from Leading Aircraftman Joe Roddis, a flight mechanic with 234 Squadron:

I'd do a pre-flight exam on the engine to see that we'd missed nothing, to see the oil tank was full, that there was 85 gallons of petrol in the tank, that everything was all right in the cockpit. Then they'd bring the aircraft to readiness. When the aircraft returned, I'd refuel the engine and put oil in it. If there was a snag and it was within my capability to fix it, I would, and then I'd run it up to see that I'd resolved the problem. I would always do an 'afterflight'. That meant giving the engine a real good going over. You might look at it and think that nothing's happened but a bullet could have gone through the cowling or the propeller. It would take about half an hour and they'd bring us back on readiness when all the other trades had finished their jobs.

Some people's jobs took longer than others. The instrument man had to replace the oxygen bottles. The radio man had to check such a lot. The rigger had responsibility for the wheels, tyres, airframe and the hood. He had to polish the hood so much; if there was a speck on the hood, it could be mistaken for a German aircraft. They were very keen on polishing that hood. So the rigger was running around with a cloth and polish.

And this is Fred Roberts, an armourer with 19 Squadron, giving an idea of the speed of operational work:

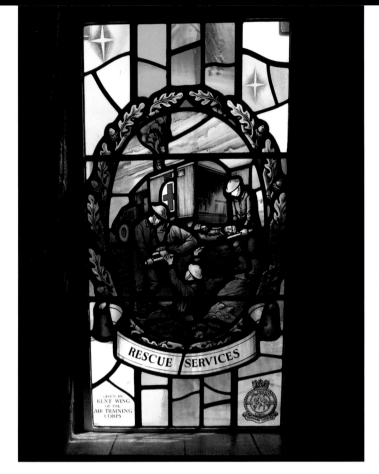

left
St George's Chapel window:
Rescue services

right
St George's Chapel window:
Parachute packing

There were red patches over the gun ports to stop the guns freezing up in high altitudes. When the aircraft came back and the red patches were gone, we'd say, 'Something's happened!' but we didn't know what until the intelligence officer had finished talking to the pilot. Unless the pilot held up one or two fingers to us.

If he'd fired the guns, I'd take the empty ammunition tanks out and put new ammunition tanks in. While I was doing that, the assistant cleaned the barrel out. When we were all done, we put the panels back on the plane, and that was it. It would take two armourers and two assistants about three and a half minutes to re-arm a Spitfire. We loaded 300 rounds into each gun. So a full re-arm was 2,400 rounds. Every squadron prided themselves on being able to rearm a Spitfire quick.

After the planes took off, you'd either have a game of football, a game of cards, or put your head down and sleep on the grass.

Jon Tan, in his book *Aces, Airmen and the Biggin Hill Wing*, tells the story of his grandfather, Raymond Davies, an armourer at Biggin Hill in 1941–2. Davies was a miner's son, born in Glamorgan in 1920. He left school at 14 and worked as a grocer's assistant until October 1940, when he volunteered for the Royal Air Force. After medical tests and basic training at RAF Bridgnorth, he was posted south. 'There were six of us who were detailed to go to Biggin Hill, Kent, and the sergeant told us what a famous station Biggin Hill was... We six were extremely privileged and excited to be posted there.'

They arrived on the night of 18th February 1941, crossing London from Paddington to Bromley by lorry during a bombing raid. When they arrived, they found 'The billets

Biggin Hill, 1943. An armourer adjusts one of the machine guns on a Spitfire Mark IX. The gun harmonisation board in front of the aeroplane marked the point of convergence of fire from the two sets of guns. This was usually set at 250 yards. The tail was jacked up to create the correct flying angle of 2 degrees down.

were lovely... We had good showers and baths... so many beds one side, and so many the other ... A proper barracks.' As they sat around the stove talking to an old hand that night, 'the Germans came over and started to bomb, and this chap jumped up quick and he says, "Ay up, let somebody run who can run!" but we were dead tired after the travelling and so stayed put.'

Biggin Hill was still badly smashed up from the previous summer, but next morning they could see fresh bomb craters scattered across the airfield and an air-raid shelter that had taken a direct hit. 'We wanted to get in and help with the clear up but they didn't want us. We weren't geared up ... The personnel that they had were experienced in clearing the 'drome up and within a matter of hours you didn't know that a bomb had dropped. That's how efficient the machine was, and it didn't interfere with aircraft getting off. If you tried to interfere, you'd get told to hop it and you soon learned not to get involved and get on with your own job.'

They were assigned as armourers' assistants in 3034 Servicing Echelon, a support team for the squadrons stationed there — at that time 74, 92 and 609. Davies was assigned to 92. Their particular job was improving the performance of the 20mm Hispano-Suiza cannon that were now being fitted to all Spitfires, with 92 Squadron receiving the first of the modified aircraft.

The cannon, with its armour-piercing shells, was far more destructive than the Browning 0.303 machine guns that had been used in the Battle of Britain, but it had problems: the ammunition feed mechanism was unreliable, as was the ejection of spent shell-cases, and the recoil settings needed continual adjustment: 'We couldn't get enough recoil in the gun in order to clear the chamber quick enough for the next round.' A special team was set up to resolve these problems. Davies and his five companions were on it, together with two armourers from 609 Squadron. In charge was Flight Sergeant Ronald 'Jimmy' Stewart of 92 Squadron, who would later be promoted to Chief Armaments Officer for 11 Group.

'By Christ did we spend a lot of time on the butts!' Davies recalled. 'The Spitfire flew two degrees nose down, so we used to put it up on the trestles and get the spirit level two degrees flying down. Then we used to have a big heavy ball – it was specially made … one each side. We used to shove the rope over and hang these, and then two of us blokes each side would hang on to the tail … And with all that bloody weight – and especially when they got going – oh the vibration, the way it shook! We had to hang on or it would have gone up in the air!'

Meanwhile the squadrons continued to fly, three or four sorties a day, often in poor weather, to protect convoys in the Channel or attack enemy targets in France. Keeping the aircraft in working condition took up much of the armourers' time, so the cannon project had to be set aside for evenings and late nights, prompting the Commanding Officer one night at 2 am to 'send a message out to the site to pack it in. After a hard day's flying nobody could get any sleep.'

The team's experiments went on through the spring and summer of 1941: firing, measuring, adjusting, firing again. The sergeant would shout, 'Another quarter turn off the recoil reducer, Davies.' Leaving his post on the tail, Davies would go to the cannon and make the adjustment with a special spanner.

As the days grew longer and the weather improved, the operational side of the work increased:

'We were dawn till dusk… If the squadron was on readiness, we had to be down the dispersal at dawn. The kites were on readiness so we had to be there as well. Then on top of that we'd have to do a duty crew every third night… We'd have time off to have our meals: B flight would stand in for us, and then we'd stand in for them when they went. … The chiefy [Flight Sergeant] always had a chart and he would allocate… "Oh Davies, you work with so-and-so today." Or sometimes you wouldn't be assigned to anybody so you'd have to do general maintenance, cleaning the guns and so on.'

In September 1941, a week of bad weather grounded the squadrons. The armourers were able to work on the cannon. Stewart now reported fewer stoppages. Yet problems persisted with the recoil and ejection mechanism. It was one of the armourers who thought of a solution. As Davies explained it, 'The 20mm system was a combination of recoil spring and gas-assistance. When the gun fired, some of the exhaust gases were channelled through a small hole into the chamber, assisting the return of the breech-block to its starting position. Well we couldn't get enough gas and so all of the adjustment in recoil had to be done with the recoil reducer at the front of the gun. And we were on the limits with this adjustment. Then one evening Corporal Jones had an idea to enlarge the hole — and made up a special drill, smaller than anything available — and the next day he took out a sliver of metal from this hole for the exhaust gases. Then we tried it out and it was just what was needed.'

Later that year, a belt-feed mechanism replaced the ammunition drum and the cannon became more reliable, its firing rate raised from 600 to 750 rounds per minute.

Meanwhile the armourers were alerted to another problem by Robert Stanford Tuck, who had been appointed Wing Commander Flying at Biggin Hill in November 1941. While chatting with the armourers one day, Tuck complained that he never knew how much ammunition he had left during combat. It was infuriating to get yourself into a perfect firing position only to hear nothing but the hiss of compressed air when you pressed the button. Davies and his friend Pete Long, an electrician, placed a pair of electrical contacts at the back of the cannon's breech, which they connected to a counter in the cockpit. Every time the block returned after firing a round it would touch the contact and complete the circuit. Tuck tried it out on a test flight. 'He said it was just what we needed and that he was going to contact Group HQ and the Air Ministry to tell them of our invention and recommend that it be adopted as a proper modification for all cannon-armed fighters.'

A week later, Tuck was shot down. He spent the next two years as a prisoner of the Germans, and Davies never knew if his recommendation was made.

The armourers worked long hours under strict discipline. Evenings off were spent in local pubs: the King's Arms at Leaves Green, the Old Jail at Biggin Hill, or the Bell in Bromley. A pass was required to leave the base, but once in a while Davies and his friends would slip through a gap in the fence for an illicit night out.

One night in February 1942, on the way back from such an escapade, they were caught. After a 'right bollocking' from the Station Commander, Philip Barwell, Davies was removed from squadron duties and made to work through a backlog of paperwork on Sgt Stewart's desk: job sheets, amendments to manuals and servicing procedures, reports on modifications, filing... 'It was crafty of Stewart,' said Davies; 'he hated this paperwork and it had been lying around for some months.' Still, Davies counted himself lucky. He could have been sent away to the 'glasshouse' (a dreaded experience), but his good record saved him.

After a week of boredom, staring out of the window and longing to get back to work, he was released for more urgent business: on 12th February 1942 squadrons all over southern England were in action over the Channel trying to stop the German warships *Gneisenau*, *Scharnhorst* and *Prinz Eugen* as they made their dash from Brest to their home port of Kiel.

The next day, Davies was told that his 'fizzer' (punishment) was over. He also learned that before his misdemeanour he had been recommended for promotion. Sgt Stewart handed him the insignia of Leading Aircraftman and told him to sew them on to his uniform at once.

There was trust and respect between ground crews and pilots, but a distance was maintained. Stanford Tuck was an exceptional character who combined social ease and film-star looks with leadership and a brilliant combat record. He could talk on equal terms with anyone. Ted Webb, of 92 Squadron's ground crew, said of him:

Donald Kingaby, the clergyman's son from North London, described by the press as 'the 109 Specialist' after shooting down four Messerschmitt 109s in one day. Kingaby was a sergeant pilot with 92 Squadron at BIggin Hill in 1940-1. He was later promoted to officer rank. By the end of the war his personal score was 21 confirmed victories, 2 shared, 6 probables and 11 damaged.

'He fought well and he lived well. He was that type. And he gave confidence to everybody.' When he failed to return from a sortie, on 28th January 1942, 'the squadron was very depressed - like losing a wheel on the motorway. The next day the Flight Sergeant comes flying down... The Station Commander said, "Right, lads, I've got a communiqué here from the German High Command: *Wing Commander Stanford Tuck is a prisoner of war in German hands.*" Talk about a goal at Wembley!'

Camaraderie was more likely between ground crews and sergeant pilots, who had come up through the ranks. Raymond Davies had particularly fond memories of Don Kingaby, a vicar's son from London and a well-known fighter ace:

It was Don Kingaby's aircraft, QJ-V, that I was assigned to when with 92 Squadron. His full-time fitter was a chap called Thomas — another Welshman. So Thomas and I got to know each other very well working on Kingaby's aircraft. He was a sergeant pilot then, and was one of the top pilots of the Wing... I think he had about twelve confirmed already, and many more unconfirmed that he was sure of ... He was a great pilot and would often shout to us when we'd got a wagon into Bromley or Croydon and would jump in the back with us. He loved the squadron, and was always great with us. He wouldn't take a commission because he knew it would mean a posting away from 92. So he ended up with three DFMs — the only pilot to have three — before they forced him to accept [a commission] and his own squadron.

Brian Kingcome tells a story that shows how strong such relationships could be. While 92 Squadron was operating from the forward station of Manston, Kingcome lent his car to his fitter, Snowy, 'a first-class technician who was a most likeable young man. He had for a long time been getting me safely into the air and down again, while also servicing and maintaining my car.'

One night Snowy parked the car outside the police station with no lights on and facing in the wrong direction: a serious hazard in the blackout. Even worse, they had found 100-octane petrol, strictly reserved for aircraft, in the tank. The Station Commander, an officious type, sent Snowy under military escort to Kingcome with the expectation of a court martial, a month or two in the glasshouse, and the end of his career in the RAF. As acting CO of the Squadron, Kingcome had to decide Snowy's fate: 'Either I could wreck the career and possibly the livelihood of a first-class mechanic whose skills were a basic resource to the squadron, or else I could deflate the ego of a small-minded senior officer who apparently thought the path to promotion was lined by a set of shiny buttons and topped off with a crisp haircut....

'I put on the most magisterial air I could muster. "I have given this case much thought," I said, "and I'm not entirely satisfied that the charges are based on a suffi-

ciently thorough examination of the facts. I have therefore decided to give the prisoner the benefit of the doubt and dismiss the case on the grounds of lack of evidence... He is to be released immediately and returned to his unit to continue with normal duties. Case closed.'"

Kingcome expected to be reprimanded for this decision. The Station Commander 'was free to question my judgement, even my sanity, but never the legality of my action. Once a case is dismissed it can never be reopened. Snowy was safe.'

Whatever the social distance, the bonds of loyalty between pilots and ground crew were strong. As Kingcome puts it, Snowy 'was a valued member of the squadron, and the squadron was family; blood was thicker than water and 92 looked after its own.' [28]

Raymond Davies expressed the ground crew's view in these words:'When our pilots took off, without any hesitation I used to salute those men away. Because, God, it's no exaggeration of the guts that those lads, those men had. They were only the same age as myself — twenty years of age, just left grammar school some of them ... entering university ... and having to dedicate their lives to fight and die for their country.'

The last year of the War

In the Spring of 1944 the last fighter squadrons were posted away from Biggin Hill and the station was designated No 22 Balloon Centre for the defence of London against flying bombs. Two hundred balloon emplacement sites had been selected along the

left
A German V2 flying bomb. This example was captured at the end of the war and shipped to Biggin Hill as part of the RAF's Reserve Collection of Historic Aircraft.

right
A barrage balloon, one of hundreds anchored on high ground in the southeast of England to protect against flying bombs in the spring and summer of 1944. Biggin Hill was designated No 22 Balloon Centre for the defence of London.

BRYAN DE GRIMEAU —
'TOWERHEAD' BIGGIN HILL — 1945.

North Downs, and No 5344 Airfield Construction Wing moved in to Biggin Hill to build access roads, anchorages, hard standings, camps and hydrogen depots. They also laid over 1,000 miles of telephone cable. Three Balloon Squadrons (945/7, 953 and 958) arrived, and the balloons were delivered by lorry from Glasgow on 16th June 1944. Three days later there were 344 of them floating on steel cables above the villages of Brasted, Westerham, Tatsfield and Ide Hill, with winches and tents in the fields below. Biggin Hill had a staff of 519 airmen to handle the balloons while 177 WAAFs took care of the transport, collecting hydrogen cylinders from Hayes station, delivering water and food to the balloon sites, and driving ambulances. The V1 flying bomb attacks lasted ten weeks, during which 8,500 bombs were launched, 2,400 of them reaching London. Biggin Hill lay at the heart of 'Doodlebug Alley' and took its share of strikes, with damage to buildings and injuries to people. Three men died when a V1 hit the Nissen hut where they were sleeping at 5.30 a.m. on 1st July 1944.

On 5th September, the attacks over, the balloons were brought down and moved to Southend, where they were deployed against flying bombs launched from aircraft over the North Sea. Later that month, Biggin Hill took on a new role as the distribution centre for Canadian forces' mail for Europe, manned by No 168 (Heavy Transport) Squadron of the Royal Canadian Air Force. In the words of Graham Wallace, 'Britain's premier fighter station was now a post office.'[29]

A few last missions, flown in October and November 1945, delivered penicillin to Warsaw, where, after five and a half years of German occupation and neglect, typhus and tuberculosis were rife. The war in Europe may have been over, but its consequences were not.

'This is where we won the war'. Sketch by Bryan de Grineau of the deserted Biggin Hill Operations Room in September 1945. Since the bombing raids of 1940 the Ops Room had been relocated to Towerfield House, Keston. Published in *The Illustrated London News*, 29.9.1945.

1   *A Willingness To Die*, Epilogue

2   See Daniel Todman, *Britain's War. Into battle 1937–1941*, Chapter 11.

3   This, at least, is how it felt at the time. Later historians, writing at a comfortable distance from the events, have discovered that the Germans were ill-prepared for an invasion and knew it, as did Churchill, who used the threat as a means of rousing the nation. Evidence for this view is given in R.J. Evans, *The Third Reich at War* (112-3) and Max Hastings, *All Hell Let Loose* (Ch 4).

4   Wallace, *RAF Biggin Hill*, 126

5   Neville Duke, *Test Pilot*, 48–9. Duke served at Biggin Hill with 92 Squadron in 1941. Although he was not a Battle of Britain pilot, the combat he describes took place just a few months later in very similar conditions.

6   Brian Kingcome, *A Willingness to Die*, 270. The pianist was Bob Holland, who survived the war but was killed soon afterwards in a flying accident. Kingcome remembers him with special fondness:'He would often take over the piano-stool from night-club pianists on our nights off, and sit there, a large drink standing by on the piano top, his eyes half closed and screwed up against the smoke from the inevitable cigarette that dangled from the corner of his mouth, fingers flitting deftly over keys he hardly seemed to touch. Whenever old tunes are revived, including 92's favourite number, 'In the Mood', I am back to hearing them endlessly teased out by Bob Holland's magic fingers... The evocation never grows less and the appeal is there for ever.' (*A Willingness to Die*, 136–7)

7   JA Kent, *One of the Few*, Ch 7 (2020 edition p 179)

8   Felicity Peake, *Pure Chance*, 36–7

9   Felicity Peake, *Pure Chance*, 43

10 Felicity Peake, *Pure Chance*, 39

11 Felicity Peake, *Pure Chance*, 41–2

12 According to Civil Defence records, over 10,000 bombs fell on Biggin Hill and the surrounding area (Westerham Hill to Keston) between 30 July 1940 and 27 March 1945: High Explosive (646), Incendiary (9742), Parachute Mine (7), Oil Bomb (17), Flying Bomb (38). Information collected from Bromley Archives by Geoff Parmakis of Biggin Hill Memorial Museum.

13 There is a list of squadrons that served at Biggin Hill in Appendix 1.

14 Brian Kingcome, *A Willingness to Die*, 135

15 Wallace, *RAF Biggin Hill*, 211-2

16 JA Kent, *One of the Few*; Brian Kingcome, *A Willingness to Die*

17 Wallace, *RAF Biggin Hill*

18 Neville Duke, *War Diaries*, 2 April 1941

19 Churchill's country house, Chartwell, lies 7 miles to the South. He used Chartwell extensively in the 1930s and 1950s, but visited only twice during the war as it was regarded as vulnerable to attack.

20 Barwell's modest, urbane manner is evident in a short interview with BBC radio which is preserved at the Imperial War Museum.

21 Wallace, 284

22 Alan Deere, *Nine Lives*, 266

23 In the heady atmosphere of the celebrations, the enormous bill for the Grosvenor House

Defending a way of life... A press photograph with pilots of 92 Squadron at Biggin Hill in 1940.

dinner (£2,500) was left unpaid. In September a new Station Intelligence Officer, Squadron Leader Hogben, found a deficit of £1,000 as he took up his post. He raised the money through a levy on all stations in 11 Group: 'a highly unpopular imposition with those who had not been invited to the celebration' (Wallace, 292)

24 St George's Chapel was threatened again in 2015 when the Ministry of Defence decided to close it in the interests of saving money. An outcry in Parliament led to the provision of alternative funding, both public and private.

25 See Peter Sikora, *Poles in the Battle of Britain: a Photographic Album of the Polish 'Few'* and C. Shore and C. Williams, *Aces High*. A useful website is https://listakrzystka.pl/en/

26 Alan Deere, *Nine Lives*, 257-8

27 Tom Neil, *Gun Button to Fire*, 115

28 Brian Kingcome, *A Willingness to Die*, 171-4. Wallace, 297

CHAPTER 4
CHANGING ROLES: RAF BIGGIN HILL
1945–92

Victory in Europe (VE) Day, 8th May 1945, was celebrated at Biggin Hill with a Service of Thanksgiving in St George's Chapel, an afternoon of sporting contests, and an evening dance in the Sergeants' Mess. The next day, a Victory Parade marched through Bromley, led by the bands of the Home Guard and the Royal Marines, with men and women from Biggin Hill taking part. After the Parade, the Forces were entertained at a Tea, Concert and Dance given by the Mayor of Bromley. A week later, a Station Victory Dance in the Gymnasium was attended by 800 personnel, with fancy dress and prizes for the best costumes. An enormous Victory Cake was cut by the Commanding Officer and the longest-serving WAAF on the Station.

So ended six years of war in Europe. Biggin Hill had been in the front line, its name immortalised in the life and death struggle of 1940. Years of recovery for Britain and Europe lay ahead, as ruined cities were rebuilt, war debts repaid, crimes prosecuted, troops and civilians repatriated. On 27th June the Station was transferred from Fighter Command to Transport Command, its staff occupied with flights of Dakotas by the 314th Squadron (US Army Air Force) and 168 (Royal Canadian Air Force "Mailcan") Squadron, transporting people, freight and mail between London, Europe and North Africa. In just one month, July 1945, 18,463 passengers passed through the Station; in August, another 15,000. In the first two weeks of September, nearly 1500 aircraft movements were recorded. There were currency exchange transactions too — some 400-500 per day, amounting to £300,000 in July, over £500,000 in August, and nearly £400,000 in October. RAF staff specialising in finance and accounting were brought in to handle this work.

Victory in Japan (VJ) Day, 15th August, the formal end of the Second World War, was noted as 'very quiet on camp', most people having taken their VJ-48s (passes for 48 hours leave). Soon this scenic aerodrome among woods and fields on the southern edge of London would return to its old peacetime routine: flying training, maintenance, movements of personnel, visits and inspections, parades, sporting and social fixtures. To improve the appearance of the grounds, a gardening competition was organised. A busy educational programme was established. In March 1946 the Station Commander noted that 'The Transport Command School of Domestic Science and Hairdressing are doing well', and that the Driving School would soon commence. Subjects listed for July that year are 'Maths, Languages, English, Carpentry, Shorthand, Music, Dressmaking and Needlework, Rug-making, Leatherwork, Geography, Art, Physics, Household Science' — a remarkable range of options, reflecting the variety of interests and abilities to be found on the Station, and the fact that many of the personnel would soon need to find civilian jobs.

Two squadrons of the Royal Auxiliary Air Force, 600 (City of London) and 615 (County of Surrey), were stationed at RAF Biggin Hill from 1946 to 1957. They flew Spitfires until 1950, then converted to Gloster Meteors – the RAF's first jet fighters.

Hawker Hunters of 41 Squadron, which were kept on
readiness at Biggin Hill from 1955 to 1958.

previous page
Detail of the altar frontal, St George's Memorial Chapel, Biggin Hill, showing the badge of the Royal Air Force with its motto Per ardua ad astra ("Through adversity to the stars"). The altar is shown in context on page 111.

Squadron Leader Frederick Sowrey, Officer Commanding 615 Squadron, briefing pilots at Biggin Hill in 1953.

Memories of the war were still vivid, and a Battle of Britain Open Day was held on 20th September 1947. Winston Churchill was guest of honour, and despite heavy rain during the later stages of the display, a crowd of 50,000 attended.

The Cold War

After a brief interval of peace, mistrust between the capitalist West and the communist East, buried since 1941 in the interests of defeating Hitler, began to resurface. The North Atlantic Treaty Organisation (NATO) was created in 1949 and the stand-off known as the 'Cold War' began. This was an undeclared state of hostility which stopped short of direct fighting. Both sides possessed nuclear weapons, whose terrible power had been demonstrated in the bombing of Hiroshima and Nagasaki in 1945, where just two bombs had killed almost a quarter of a million people. Rather than risk annihilation by nuclear attack, both sides in the Cold War preferred to operate indirectly — through espionage, propaganda, economic embargoes, sporting and

below

The main runway of Biggin Hill, showing the Operational Readiness Platforms (ORPs) built for Cold War fighter jets alongside each end.

right

An aerial view of Biggin Hill three years after the Second World War. Note the 'E-pens' for dispersal of fighter aircraft around the airfield, and the Officers' Mess with its formal gardens (two thirds up on the left).

technological rivalry, the space race, and proxy wars fought in third world countries with conventional weapons. A 'balance of terror' was maintained, containment was the aim, and sobering acronyms like MAD (Mutual Assured Destruction) kept national leaders and military chiefs committed to compromise.

Meanwhile, military technology continued to develop. Ballistic missiles of steadily increasing destructive capability, launched from aircraft, submarines or terrestrial sites, were changing the nature of warfare. A regular RAF squadron, No 41, arrived in 1951, equipped with Meteor VIIIs, then (in 1955) with Hawker Hunter F5s. The main runway was extended, with areas of hard standing at each end known as ORPs — Operational Readiness Platforms —where jet fighters would sit ready to take off at two minutes' notice. Now Biggin Hill was back on first-line status for the first time since 1945.

On 19th January 1951, the Australian Prime Minister, Robert Menzies, visited Biggin Hill to christen a new jet bomber, the Canberra, in the presence of senior British and American Air Force officers and the chairman of the manufacturing company, English Electric Aircraft. The company's chief test pilot, Ronald Beaumont, gave a flying display in this remarkable new aircraft.

In July 1951 Lord Dowding, who had led Fighter Command during the Battle of Britain, laid the foundation stone for the new St George's Memorial Chapel at Biggin Hill. (An earlier chapel, assembled from three prefabricated huts in 1943, had been destroyed by fire in 1946.) The dedication ceremony, on 10th November 1951, was led by the Bishop of Rochester, in the company of the Secretary of State for Air and other distinguished guests. Intended as a permanent memorial to the 454 aircrew who lost their lives while serving at RAF Biggin Hill in the Second World War, its fine stained glass windows and oak reredos, its emblems, squadron standards and Book of Remembrance have kept their memory alive in an atmosphere of quiet recollection

above
Re-arming a Meteor 8 of 615 Squadron, Biggin Hill 1952.

right
Sir Robert Gordon Menzies, Australian Prime Minister, christens the English Electric Canberra, Biggin Hill, 19th January 1951.The Canberra was the RAF's first jet-powered bomber. It was named after the capital of Australia, which was the first foreign country to buy the aircraft. Conceived as a successor to the de Havilland Mosquito, it served for more than 50 years with air forces around the world.

left
Wing Commander James Wallace, who led the Royal Air Force fly-past of 168 aircraft for the Coronation of Queen Elizabeth II on 2nd June 1953. The picture was taken during a rehearsal at Biggin Hill in May.

right
The altar and reredos of St George's Memorial Chapel, Biggin Hill.

for over 70 years. Sir Winston Churchill, who led the fundraising campaign for its construction, wrote, 'As a nation we have short memories and it is well that memorials such as this should bring to our remembrance the cost of victory in the days when one of our fighter pilots had to be worth ten. They died without seeing the reward of their efforts; we live to hold their reward inviolate and unfading'.

In 1953 Wing Commander Denis ('Splinters') Smallwood arrived as Station Commander. He had flown Hurricanes and Spitfires in the war, and received the Distinguished Flying Cross for his part in the Dieppe Raid of 1942. His citation for the Distinguished Service Order (1944) spoke of 'the highest standard of skill and gallantry in air operations... By his great tactical ability, fine fighting qualities and gallant leadership, he has contributed materially to the successes obtained. In addition to his work in the air, Wing Commander Smallwood has devoted much of his technical knowledge towards the training of other members of the squadron with good results. His devotion to duty has been unfailing.'

Smallwood's energy and leadership quickened the pace of life on the Station. The At Home Day in September featured flying and static displays, a fun fair, and some inspired special attractions: a children's train, practice bombing with electrically controlled model aircraft ("threepence per bomb and a there is a prize for a direct hit"), aerobatics on request ("On payment of sixpence at the kiosk in front of the Control Tower you can speak to the pilot of a Chipmunk, who will perform any manoeuvre, within limits (!) that you ask for"), and an offer that no schoolboy could resist, Have Your Photograph Taken as a Fighter Pilot: "The map on the back page shows where

you can find a Meteor on the firing butts. For two shillings you can fire two or three rounds from a 20mm cannon and have your photograph taken in the cockpit. The print will be sent to you within the next two days." A Foreword in the Open Day Programme sounded a friendly note: "Every officer and airman on this Station is here today to look after you. Do not hesitate to ask questions. We hope that you enjoy yourselves and find much to interest you. Welcome." The day attracted 170,000 visitors, and raised £900 for the RAF Benevolent Fund.

All ranks, with the Station Commander's encouragement, were reported to be taking a great interest in station sports. Wednesday afternoons 'are reserved for games of every description, and everyone must take part... The Officers' Mess Squash Court, re-opened after being under repair for some considerable time, is for the use of all ranks on Wednesdays.' Smallwood had an eye for everyone under his command, junior as well as senior: a Corporals Club was opened in December 1954, and the Sergeants were entertained to a games evening in the Officers' Mess.

It was a special honour for the Station when, on 15th May 1954 the Biggin Hill Wing, led by Smallwood, flew at the head of 180 aircraft in formation over the Thames Estuary to welcome the Queen and the Duke of Edinburgh as they returned from a Commonwealth Tour on board the Royal Yacht *Britannia*. Official visitors to Biggin Hill included the French Prime Minister, Pierre Mendès France, who was met by Winston Churchill and Anthony Eden on 23rd August 1954. The Shah of Iran visited on 22nd February 1955, and Queen Elizabeth the Queen Mother on 23rd April 1955.

left
Programme cover for the RAF At Home Day 1953.

right
Queen Elizabeth the Queen Mother visits the Memorial Chapel at Biggin Hill on St George's Day (23rd April) 1955. With her is the Revd Vivian Symons, Vicar of Biggin Hill and the Chapel's first Chaplain. Behind them is the Station Commander, Wing Commander Denis 'Splinters' Smallwood.

At a ceremony on 15th December 1955 the Borough of Bromley formally 'adopted' RAF Biggin Hill. The Mayor, Thomas Baylis, spoke of 'the people's gratitude for the part played by the Station during the Battle of Britain' and presented an illuminated manuscript to the Commandant, who replied with a speech about the historic connection with the Borough, emphasising 'how necessary it was for the armed forces to have full civil backing both in peace and war.' He then presented a Station badge to the Council. Drinks and music followed.

Smallwood's vision went wider. In 1953 he decided to commission a history of RAF Biggin Hill, and gave his Education Officer, Flight Lieutenant TA Lycett, the task of searching the official records and collecting personal memories from men and women who had served there or lived in the villages nearby. This was well timed: 36 years had passed since the first aeroplane landed at Biggin Hill in 1917, and the early days were already fading from memory. Advertisements in the press produced letters from former officers, airmen and cadets. There was even a reply from Mrs Westacott, whose husband had farmed the land before it became an airfield. Together with official documents, these recollections were skilfully shaped into a narrative by Graham Wallace. His book, *RAF Biggin Hill* was published in 1957. It remains a vivid and highly readable account.

Another important act of preservation took place with the formation at Biggin Hill of the Battle of Britain Memorial Flight (named at that time the Historic Aircraft Flight). Its first four aeroplanes — a Hurricane and three Spitfires — arrived on 11th

July 1957. The Spitfires were flown by Battle of Britain pilots Johnnie Johnson, Jamie Rankin and Peter Thompson (Officer Commanding RAF Biggin Hill)[2]. Meanwhile another group of aeroplanes, captured from the enemy or surrendered during the Second World War, was stored at Biggin as part of the RAF's Reserve Collection of Historic Aircraft. They included examples of flying bombs (V1 and V2), the Junkers 88, Messerschmitt 109 and 110, Focke-Wulf 190, Heinkel 111, Fiat CR 42, and Mitsubishi Ki-46. In the late 1960s they were moved from Biggin Hill to RAF St Athan, and later into the RAF Museum's collections at Hendon and Cosford.

Biggin Hill continued to operate as an active fighter station until 1958, with 41 Squadron in full-time residence and and the two Auxiliary squadrons, 600 and 615, at weekends. John Hext was a Hunter pilot on 41 Squadron, who served at Biggin Hill from 1956 to 1958. Their role, he recalls, was air defence exercises: 'protecting our borders and our skies, investigating anybody who got too close. On PIs (practice interceptions) somebody would go up and act as the enemy and we would act as the interceptor looking for him and then do a dummy attack using our ciné guns. If you were on standby for an exercise or the possibility of a threat of any sort you were invariably out on the ORP, which was a designated area very close to the edge of the runway where you would sit close by the aircraft in a little hut, or if you were on high readiness alert in the cockpit, and that I can assure you is not fun. Normally you would sit in there for an hour at least, maybe more, waiting to be called. It was hot and you hoped you would get called soon because you wouldn't be in a fit state after two hours. You were all strapped in, you couldn't move around, strapped to the ejector seat,

previous page
Detail of the altar frontal, St George's Memorial Chapel, Biggin Hill, showing the badge of the Royal Air Force with its motto Per ardua ad astra ("Through adversity to the stars"). The altar is shown in context on page 11.

left
A Hurricane and the last three Spitfires in service with the RAF arrive at Biggin Hill to form the Historic Aircraft Flight, 11th July 1957.

above
Three Second World War fighter aces (left to right: Wing Commander PD Thompson, Group Captain James Rankin, Group Captain JE 'Johnnie' Johnson) who flew the three Spitfires in the picture on the left into Biggin Hill on 11th July 1957.

connected to the intercom, oxygen, everything. You came down soaking wet with
perspiration. It wasn't all jam and honey I can tell you...

'If you were in a hut or a tent you would walk or run to the aircraft, climb a little
ladder on the side and the ground crew man would come along behind you and help
strap you in, take the steps away and off you went. It was very much Battle of Britain
stuff. You were scrambled and given a vector to climb and a frequency to connect with
and from there you were guided to the enemy. We did this all the time, every day. We
used to intercept things like American bombers, or Vulcans or Valiants, or Victors, maybe
50 miles away at 40,000 feet. The GCIs (Ground Control Interception centres), which
were all below ground, would guide you via radar straight to where the aircraft was.
You would look for the target, and when you saw it you would press the button and
say to ground control, "Contact. Tally-ho!" which told ground control you then didn't
need them for guidance.'

The Squadron buildings were old prefabricated SECO huts by the side of the hangar,
with a Pilots' Room, Operations Room, and Squadron Leader's Office. Every morning
at eight the pilots reported to the main Ops Building by the Control Tower for a weather
briefing and then walked back up to the Squadron. 'You knew what sortie you were on
because it was promulgated the night before: they wrote up on the board who would
fly the first detail.'

The commanding officer of 41 was Squadron Leader James Castagnola, DFC, DSO*,
a former Lancaster pilot with a distinguished war record; among many other actions
he had taken part in the sinking of the German battleship *Tirpitz*. A slightly built, mod-

above
A Hawker Hunter 5 of 41 Squadron at Biggin Hill, c. 1956.

left
Pilots of 41 Squadron at Biggin Hill, 1956-7. Left to right: Peter Hardy, Chips Carpenter, Kenny Palmer (US Marine Corps Exchange Officer), John Hext, Peter Brown.

opposite
41 Squadron, June 1956.
Left to right (standing) Doug Rose, Craig Young, Roy Irish, John Lancaster, Jim Vigar; (in chairs) Stan Barnes, John Hext, Kenny Palmer, Benjy Britton, James Castagnola, Dave Harris, Richard Pratt, Colin Thompson, Sq Ldr Carson (visiting), John Collins; (on ground) Roger Coulston, Peter Wright.

est man, liked and respected by the squadron, he never spoke about his wartime flying. Nor did the Station Commander, Wing Commander Peter Thompson DFC, a Battle of Britain pilot. 'You would never ask the senior officers about the War,' says Hext. 'You held them in reverence for what they'd gone through. Many of us used to say we wished we were a few years older so that we could have done what they did, but you couldn't really say that: we could just as easily have been killed.'

Biggin Hill in the 1950s was a pleasant place to serve, 'the only station in the Air Force,' says Hext, 'which had its own outdoor swimming pool. I was married then and we had our first son there. I was only a pilot officer and I got a married quarter, which was unheard of at other stations. You had to have lots of points for length of service normally, but luckily at Biggin there were plenty of houses and we got a married quarter within a couple of months. My son was born in '57, and christened in the Memorial Chapel.

'To me it was a great honour to be there. Biggin Hill was synonymous with the Battle of Britain, and I was always very aware, very thrilled and very honoured to follow in the footsteps. I pride myself on having done a tour in one of the most famous

fighter stations in the Air Force. I loved my time there, and could have stayed for ever.'

Unfortunately 'for ever' was not an option. In 1957 the Government's White Paper on Defence, known as the Sandys Review, announced that the changing nature of warfare and the state of the nation's economy required a reduction in the armed forces and the replacement, in due course, of the fighter force with ground to air guided missiles. Biggin Hill's days as a military airfield were numbered.That same year the Royal Auxiliary Air Force was disbanded, as was 41 Squadron in January 1958. On 8th February 1959, the Operations Record Book noted that 'all Royal Air Force flying ceased from the Station.'

It is well known, and not just in the RAF, that shutting down a great project is an emotional business. Even more so a whole community: all that history, all those lives... The decision to stop flying from Biggin Hill must have been very reluctantly taken. Economic and strategic assessments are unsentimental, however, and a fighter station in the south-eastern corner of London, having been in the right place at the right time for 30 years of national crisis, was now no longer needed.

Biggin Hill was assigned a new role under Training Command. In 1959 the Ground Officers Selection Centre was transferred from Uxbridge, followed by the Aircrew Selection Centre from Hornchurch in 1962, and the RAF Selection Board from Cranwell in 1964. In a smart set of new buildings these three bodies formed the Officers and Aircrew Selection Centre, to interview and test applicants to the service, assessing their physical, mental and temperamental fitness for a career in the RAF.

above

Hawker Hunters of 41 Squadron, stationed at Biggin Hill from 1955 to 1958. The Hunter was the Royal Air Force's principal fighter aircraft in the years 1954 to 1960. It was the first jet designed and built by Hawker Aircraft, which had produced the Hurricane in the 1930s and 40s. Neville Duke, a fighter pilot who served at Biggin Hill, was Hawker's main test pilot after the Second World War.

The Officers and Aircrew Selection Centre

A staff of 60 worked at the new Officers and Aircrew Selection Centre under the command of an Air Commodore. They included secretarial and planning staff, medical board members and 'boarding officers' (i.e. examiners) who did a tour of two years, with a few retired officers staying longer for continuity. Food, housekeeping, transport, medical facilities and other support for the busy OASC personnel were provided by a separate station establishment of about 200 under a Wing Commander.

Over 30 years the OASC processed candidates not only for the RAF but also for the Fleet Air Arm and the Army Air Corps: a total of 210,773 went through between April 1962 and July 1992. Target figures for recruitment would rise and fall over the years, with a marked decrease after the collapse of the Soviet Union in 1990 — the so-called 'Peace Dividend'. With an average of some 7,000 candidates per year, 140 per week, work at the Centre was unceasing.

The assessment process, referred to as 'boarding', lasted two to three days, and consisted of a medical examination, aptitude tests, an interview and practical team-work exercises. Interviewers received careful guidance. They were advised to establish a 'friendly, sympathetic but detached relationship' with the candidates in order to 'put them at ease, gain their confidence and persuade them to talk freely and frankly about themselves'. An interview should be a 'controlled and purposeful conversation' but 'not an interrogation'. A chronological sequence of questions was asked, with special emphasis on the last ten years (work and family for older candidates, school or uni-

versity for younger ones). In making evaluations, interviewers were required to be as objective, fair and thorough as possible, to be acutely aware of their own prejudices, and to understand that 'even the best interview has inevitable shortcomings, because by its very nature it is a subjective situation'. On the other hand 'conscientiousness, alertness and humility on the part of the interviewer' could mitigate these shortcomings.

For the practical exercises, candidates wore overalls with a large number on the chest and back, which gave them anonymity while allowing easy identification. The exercises were designed to reveal qualities of character and temperament through challenging role-plays. One that many recruits remember is the task of taking a team across a tank of water infested with imaginary alligators, using oil drums, ropes and a plank of wood. Boarding officers marked each candidate on the quality of their contribution to the exercise, whether as leaders or as members of the team.

Candidates were marked on a wide range of qualities. *Personality* included appearance, bearing, courtesy, enthusiasm, composure, clarity of expression, and sense of humour. Under *Character* ('of utmost importance in the search for potential leaders') were qualities such as determination, integrity, courage and sense of responsibility, while *Temperament* included imagination, judgement, co-operation, clarity and logic in thinking, and breadth of outlook.

Graham Pitchfork was Officer Commanding OASC at Biggin Hill, 1989–91. 'The whole purpose,' he says, 'was to meet a particular target which I was given by the Director of Royal Air Force Recruiting. I had to find about 1200 people a year. To meet that target I had to see about 6500 candidates. We would hold three or four boards per week, with about 30 candidates per board. Each of these boards had a number of

Wing Commanders and Squadron Leaders, and they would take a proportion of those candidates. So there would be five groups of six and each pair of Wing Commanders and Squadron Leaders would be responsible for one group. The boarding officers were overseen by their Group Captain, who would wander in and out of the sessions to get a feel for who the candidates were. Once they'd been there two days we had a pretty strong indication of who the likely successes were going to be. There was a halfway stage when I would get involved as well: if there were some particularly good candidates I would drop in and have a look at how they were getting along.'

On top of the 'regular' boards of air and ground personnel OASC had a number of other assessments to make. 'Everybody who wanted to get a university scholarship or bursary from the RAF would come to us and we would take them through the same system. That was helpful because it gave us a feeling for what numbers and quality we would get downstream, three years later.' They also assessed candidates for Flying Scholarships — civilian flying lessons sponsored by the RAF and awarded to promising 16 year-olds — and each year they held 'a stimulating few days when we invited disabled individuals to come to Biggin to compete for Flying Scholarships sponsored by King Hussein of Jordan'.

The 'boarding' system was carefully thought out and soon became renowned. It brought observers from airlines, breweries, schools and a host of foreign air forces: US, Italian, Egyptian, South African, Greek, Brazilian, Indian, Thai, and many more. Of course good systems need constant monitoring, and this too was built in. Boarding officers were warned against judging candidates too quickly or superficially, too generously or harshly. Other common errors included the 'halo effect' — 'one outstandingly "good" or "bad" quality in a person casting its reflection upon all judgements pertaining to him'. (As an example of the halo effect, the advice quotes 'the common belief that healthy, neat individuals with smiling faces are necessarily intelligent'.)

left
Cadets of 2427 Squadron Air Training Corps on parade at Biggin Hill, 29th June 2022.

Candidates were assessed as completely as possible in the time available, with an exploration of family and educational background, financial circumstances, personal interests, sporting, academic and professional achievements, responsibilities, awareness of current affairs, and of the realities of Service life. Separate notes were taken of personality (defined as 'outwardly apparent traits'), character ('a person's moral strength') and temperament (revealed by 'an individual's reaction to new situations').

Boarding officers were also asked to consider educational capacity ('how the candidate will assimilate the academic side of training'), willingness to keep fit, and motivation for a career in the armed forces: 'Particular attention must be paid to the candidate's desire to join a fighting Service and the interviewer must be sure that the candidate knows what is involved and has considered all the implications.'

As time went by the boarding process had to be adjusted according to the demands of society and of the Service. 'My stay at Biggin coincided with changing times,' says Graham Pitchfork. 'The Peace Dividend affected the into-service numbers of entrants, there was an urgent need to get the navigator aptitude test upgraded from the steam age to the jet age, we started selecting females for aircrew, the Flying Scholarship scheme had to be overhauled and I had big concerns about the inflexibility of the medical standards. Add to all this the need to prepare plans to close Biggin and move the whole establishment to Cranwell...'

There were special occasions too: a 50th anniversary celebration for the Battle of Britain, with a service of thanksgiving and a dinner in the Officers' Mess with wartime fighter aces as guests, and in 1990 'a wonderful visit by eight ladies of the wartime Air Transport Auxiliary who came to see the selection process for the first female aircrew.' One of these, Diana Barnato Walker, wrote afterwards: 'It was a complete eye-opener to all of us to be in on the selection board interviews, and to be allowed to try one of the tests, and to watch the various exercises in the hangar. "I wouldn't have missed it for worlds," said one of my pilots: and I heartily agreed. No wonder all the Officers and NCOs in the RAF nowadays are such special people. What an important and wonderful task you are doing.' Her friend Margaret Frost was particularly struck by 'the great care and kindness shown towards each candidate (and you must have so many passing through), and the long hours you all seem to work. I think the Country is very lucky to have such dedicated people about.'

RAF Cadets

The first Cadet unit at Biggin Hill was a group from Bromley founded in 1938, when schoolboys helped with carrying messages, filling sandbags, cleaning aircraft and other useful tasks around the fighter station. They continued to be present throughout the Second World War, and many a local lad played a part in the struggle to keep the airfield operational through desperate times. On 5th February 1941 the Air Training

Corps was officially established with King George VI as Air Commodore-in-Chief. Post-war, girls and boys volunteered at air shows, selling programmes, providing information to the public, helping in the car parks, and, as one old hand puts it, 'going around in uniform feeling important, which all children love.'

Biggin Hill's own 2427 Squadron Air Training Corps was founded in 1964. Flight Lieutenant Andrew Simpson was Officer Commanding from 1985 to 1994. It was a busy unit, which grew from 30 to 70 members in his time and has since grown to more than 80. The cadets, aged 12 to 20, come from local schools. They are offered courses in navigation, flying and gliding, adventurous training, music, sports, leadership skills and First Aid, as well as the Duke of Edinburgh Award scheme. Cadet training is now recognised as a BTEC (Business and Technology Education Council) qualification carrying credits for university entrance.

'Most of our cadets wanted to join the RAF,' says Simpson, 'and we were able to prepare them for the tests at OASC. Not all of them passed, and our biggest problem was managing expectations. But we had a lot of successes. Mike Ling, the longest-serving Red Arrows pilot, is one of ours, and so are many senior RAF officers, medics, engineers, NCOs... They all worked hard, learned a lot and made something of themselves. Eighty percent of the RAF's intake now are Air Cadets.'

Until 1992, the cadets at Biggin Hill had 'the run of the station'. When the RAF departed, their territory was reduced to a Second World War Armoury and Parachute Store with a small parade ground and flagpole. Their commitment remained strong, however. With a staff of 18 adult volunteers, they meet twice a week under Squadron Leader John Wohlgemuth in an atmosphere of learning, enthusiasm and disciplined energy that keeps the RAF spirit alive in this historic place.

Farewell

On 31st October 1990 Air Commodore Pitchfork travelled to Lincolnshire for a ceremony to cut the first piece of turf for the new Officers and Aircrew Selection building. The decision had been made to move the Centre to Cranwell, the RAF's officer cadet school, in order to concentrate selection and training in one place — and, as ever, to reduce costs.

In July 1991 Pitchfork handed over to a new Commanding Officer, Air Commodore Peter Gover, who conducted the last Annual Formal Inspection on 5th May 1992. On 19th June a final Annual Reception was held in the Officers' Mess. 'Many military and civil dignitaries attended,' says the Operations Record Book, and 'Air Commodore Gover took the salute at a Sunset Ceremony where a flypast was performed by a single Tornado aircraft.'

So ended the 75-year story of RAF Biggin Hill: a story that, if we think of it as a single day, dawned with experiments in radio telephony, blazed through a noon of glory as a Battle of Britain fighter station, and gradually faded into an afternoon of supporting roles in peacetime. The name of Biggin Hill would live on as a symbol of heroism — that modest, good-humoured, peculiarly British heroism that shrugs off praise and insists on the team as the source of strength — but the sad fact was that by 1992 its runways and buildings were no longer needed for the defence of the nation. For the Royal Air Force, it was time to move on. As living establishments, only the Memorial Chapel and the Air Cadets remained.

Similar stories could be told of hundreds of wartime airfields. Many were abandoned and built over with factories and housing estates, which of course was a logical and productive use of the space, and a sign of the peace and prosperity that Britain has enjoyed since the Second World War. Yet something valuable is lost when an airfield closes, a spirit of enterprise and invention, of bold thinking, engineering and adventure, which are the necessary companions of aviation in all its forms. Biggin Hill was lucky enough to be spared this fate. Thanks to the efforts of some highly determined, resourceful and enthusiastic people, it survived as an airfield. As we shall see in the next chapter, it was another near-run thing.

1   The source material for Wallace's book still exists in the National Archives: AIR 20/9645 – 9649 (five Documents, with the title "Compilation of History of RAF Biggin Hill). I have used some of this material in Chapter 1 of the present book.
2   They stayed less than a year, moving to North Weald in March 1958 before taking up a more permanent home at RAF Coltishall in Lincolnshire.
3   Interview between the author and John Hext, 18th April 2022
4   This is the full list: Personality: Appearance (Build, Bearing, Deportment, Dress, Grooming, Distinctive Features), Manner (Alertness, Courtesy, Composure, Enthusiasm, Self Confidence, Sense of Humour); Powers of Expression (Clarity, Vocabulary, Fluency, Lucidity, Conviction). Character ('of utmost importance in the search for potential leaders'): Integrity, Courage, Determination, Assertiveness, Initiative, Decisiveness, Conscientiousness, Sense of Responsibility. Temperament: Imagination, Judgement, Co-operation, Loyalty, Clarity and Logic in thinking, Flexibility, Consideration for others, Breadth of Outlook.
5   Female candidates were first boarded in 1960, with much debate about suitable physical and aptitude tests. Thirty years later women began to be employed as aircrew.
6   Email to the author, 29 January 2022
7   Letters to Graham Pitchfork.

ROYAL AIR FORCE
ROYAL AIR FORCE
XX284
ROYAL AIR FORCE
L AIR FORCE

CHAPTER 5
FLYING CLUBS AND AIR SHOWS
1959-94

We must now go back 33 years: to 1959, when the RAF stopped flying at Biggin Hill. This was also the year that Croydon Airport, which had been Britain's main civilian airport since 1920, was closed.

Croydon too was a historic airfield: the headquarters of British Imperial Airways, it had the world's first air traffic control tower, airport hotel, and specially-designed terminal building. Charles Lindbergh had landed there at the end of his transatlantic crossing in *Spirit of St Louis* in 1927, and in 1930 Amy Johnson took off from Croydon for her pioneering flight to Australia, returning to a welcome from a vast crowd. It had been an important fighter station in the Battle of Britain too.

The site, however, was too small to accommodate the enormous increase in passenger traffic that was predicted, and there was no room for expansion. It was decided to re-develop the airport as housing and parkland, leaving a few relics of its old splendour: the hotel, terminal building and control tower. This decision left a collection of flying clubs, workshops and air charter companies without a home.

The Ministry of Transport and Civil Aviation went searching for a new base for these 'flying tenants'. With 22 airfields closed in the Home Counties since 1945, only one suitable location was found: Biggin Hill, nine miles to the east. Discussions were held with the Air Ministry (which controlled the RAF) about 'the possible use of some accommodation on the aerodrome on a joint-user basis'. The Croydon tenants were invited to a meeting at Biggin Hill on 22nd November 1957 'to examine the accommodation that might be offered'. Another meeting was held in January 1958, and by the end of August that year the Ministry of Transport had prepared its offer: use of the airfield, and 22 buildings in the South Camp for rent as hangars, offices and workshops. Tenants would be required to maintain the runways, roads, grass and buildings, provide all airport services, insure against losses, and indemnify the Ministry against claims. The period of lease was until 1st January 1963. The terms were far from generous, and soon led to trouble.

A group of Croydon tenants gathered around two energetic directors of Surrey Flying Club: 35 year-old Jock Maitland, an ex-fighter pilot who had flown Spitfires in the Middle East and Sabre jets with the US Air Force in Korea, and 50 year-old Edward Drewery, a builder and property developer from Sidcup, who provided the business experience and cash. 'A company is in the process of formation,' they announced, 'which all organisations that wish to go to Biggin Hill can join. The major shareholder will undertake the task of operating the airfield for the benefit of all the members. This company will undertake to run the airfield as economically as possible. The company will lease the Hangar and Airfield from the Air Ministry and hold the MTCA airfield licenses.' Annual costs, including services, rates, insurance and maintenance, were expected to be about £2,000 per company, and £50 per aeroplane.

The Air Ministry, which owned Biggin Hill, was prepared to let them try, although options were carefully kept open in case the station should be needed again for military purposes. Parts of the airfield were therefore reserved for the RAF, including the main runway and control tower. The new company, Surrey Aviation, was granted the use of runway 11/29 and areas to its north and south. Despite repeated requests for a lease, the Air Ministry delayed, pleading the 'complicated' nature of the arrangement.

Maitland and Drewery pressed on with their plans. By November 1959 a healthy collection of businesses had moved in. Jock Maitland wrote to the Under Secretary of State for Air, William Taylor MP, asking to rent more land. 'All hangar space is now occupied and aircraft owners from Croydon and elsewhere are being turned away.' Land was needed for winter parking, hangars, a public enclosure, toilets, a restaurant, and Customs facilities. Maitland went on to make another plea: 'There is a valuable opportunity to plan and control the development of Biggin Hill along systematic and practical lines but this may be lost through uncoordinated though understandable efforts on the part of individuals to satisfy their own immediate needs.'

The first request was turned down ('There is a future Defence need for the majority of the buildings and the greater part of the airfield land and this inevitably limits the facilities which can be granted for civil use'). The second was ignored, and continued to be ignored for many years.

In January 1962, 17 tenants were listed at Biggin Hill: Surrey Aviation, Seismograph Service England, the Ministry of Works, D. Dillow (a café restaurant, known inevitably as 'the Greasy Spoon'), A.J. Whittemore Aeradio Ltd, Vendair Aircraft Services and Sales, Air Touring Club, Experimental Flying Group, Biggin Hill Flying Club, Alouette Flying

previous page
The RAF Red Arrows, who appeared regularly at the Biggin Hill Air Fair from 1965.

left
Fighter ace Douglas Bader shows two young visitors (Howard and David Warner) a Fairey Swordfish at the Biggin Hill Air Fair in 1966.

above
Squadron Leader Jock Maitland DFC on his wedding day in 1952.

above
Ted Drewery (1908–84) Jock Maitland's business partner at Biggin Hill.

right
The opening of a new civilian control tower, 15th July 1960. At that time the more solid RAF tower was reserved for possible military use.

Club, Esso Petroleum Co, Air Couriers Ltd, Surrey and Kent Flying Club, Decca Air Navigation, Westerham Press, and Mr Duncan, a farmer who had Building No 68 and an 'agricultural licence for haymaking over 110 acres of airfield'.

John Allison remembers flying with the Air Touring Club at Biggin Hill in 1960, as a 17-year-old schoolboy on his way to a career in the RAF: 'They were operating from modest premises on the airfield and had two Cirrus-engined Auster Autocrats, G-AHHL and G-AHHS. The club members were very welcoming and kind and, once I had been checked out, very trusting. The club ethos was that members could take aircraft away on trips and, despite my youth, I was trusted to do that. My favourite destination was Coventry, to see my girl friend, Gill (now my wife of 56 years). The aircraft cost £3 per hour to hire.'

The first three years of Biggin Hill as a civilian airfield were in some ways a success and in other ways a failure. Drewery and Maitland bought a pair of Vickers Viscount passenger aircraft and founded Maitland Drewery Airlines, which operated from Gatwick for a few years. They had ambitious projects, including a national airline for Luxembourg (which came to nothing), and an air show which was to become one of the most successful and spectacular public events in Britain. Surrey Aviation failed to break even, but Ted Drewery was committed and had deep pockets. Jock Maitland was a determined and inspiring leader, highly regarded by all who worked with him. The partners shared a clear vision for the future of Biggin Hill as a base for private aviation — from light aircraft to business jets. There was plenty of demand, and they knew it. What they did not know, and could not possibly imagine, was that their path would be strewn with a nightmarish series of obstacles by government officials for the next 20 years.

left
Surrey and Kent Flying Club aircraft,
Biggin Hill 1964.

right
The main airport buildings in 1964.
Clockwise from lower left: the Officers'
Mess, West Camp, RAF Control Tower,
main runway, hangar and prefabricated
huts, the new Officers and Aircrew
Selection Centre, St George's Chapel.
Running through it is the Bromley-
Westerham road.

In 1961 the first lease was signed. It offered no security of tenure, which in turn discouraged investment in the fabric of the airport, its buildings and surfaces, and the installation of modern facilities. Surrey Aviation was denied full control over the tenants and airfield boundaries, so that the security and safety of aircraft operations could not be guaranteed. As a consequence, their operating license was in constant danger of being withdrawn. This precarious and uncertain arrangement continued for the next two decades, with new agreements in 1966 and 1978. It was, says Jim Maitland (Jock's son, who joined the business in 1983) 'a series of rotten deals.'

Maitland and Drewery were deeply frustrated as well as out of pocket, and their feelings are evident in the letters they wrote to a series of Government departments: the Air Ministry (absorbed by the Ministry of Defence in 1964), the Treasury Solicitor, the Ministry of Aviation (which became part of the Ministry of Technology in 1967, then the Department of Trade and Industry in 1970), and later Orpington Council (merged with the London Borough of Bromley in 1965). A typically confusing piece of civil service double-speak was sent from the Ministry of Defence on 5th October 1964: 'You felt you should not be called upon to hand back the runway extension in better condition than when taken over... In this connection I explained that the Minister has a dual role — that of Landlord and that of Licensing Authority. I would agree that as Landlord he could not reasonably expect you to carry out capital improvements during such a short tenancy. As Licensing Authority, however, he can and must insist on the runway being up to a certain standard as a condition precedent to the grant of an aerodrome licence and, of course, so maintain, or the licence could be withdrawn'. Through endless patience and negotiation the partners managed to keep the airfield open. 'Most people,' says Jim Maitland, 'would have given up.'

Not all officials were hostile, but their lives were complicated by continual renaming of departments, re-organisation of responsibilities, changes of policy, and conflicting priorities within those policies. A decision was made in 1960 to transfer half the airfield from the Air Ministry to the Ministry of Aviation, with the proviso that it could be reclaimed at short notice for Defence purposes. It took until 1963 for the

transfer to be made, and even then the title to the land remained with the Ministry of Defence. Among many complications was a Government White Paper of August 1961 announcing that all civil aerodromes would have to be self-supporting. So, while taking over the aerodrome, the Ministry of Aviation started casting about for a suitable organisation to operate it. Surrey Aviation begged for a long-term lease on Biggin Hill, and even offered to buy it outright, but the Ministry had other plans. Without explaining why, they informed Surrey Aviation: 'The disposal of the aerodrome is at present the subject of discussions between the Orpington Urban District Council and this Ministry.'[1]

These discussions, which began in 1962, were to continue for the next 12 years.

In September 1965, Jock Maitland summed up the situation in a letter to *The Kentish Times:*

The operation of Biggin hill has been my responsibility since its opening as a civil airport nearly seven years ago. At that time business was restricted to a few organisations, disgruntled and slightly demoralised after forcible eviction from Croydon — the aircraft they flew were either old or very old.

Over the intervening years a most remarkable change has taken place, almost unnoticed. Today, Biggin Hill's 100 plus resident aircraft are more modern than anything to be seen outside America. More take-offs and landings are recorded in a year than at any other airport in Europe save London's Heathrow. All this in the face of short leases and an uncertain future. One of our finest flying clubs has already been booted off two airfields since the war. Small wonder that pressure is building up, demanding to know what is to happen. The years of uncertainty have acted as a brake on business and have been tragic in the immense deterioration of the airfield's facilities.

left
A US-registered Piper Navajo in front of the Steel House, used by Jock Maitland as airport offices. The house was displayed at the 1964 Ideal Home Exhibition by Ted Drewery's building firm. Notoriously cold in winter, it was demolished in 2011.

right
A Vickers Viscount airliner. These were popular attractions at the early Biggin Hill Air Fairs.

...The operating company is and always has been willing to undertake the salvage and development of the airfield immediately, either on its own plan or on one prepared by the Ministry of Aviation or the Borough Council. Here at least flying need not constitute an added burden to the ratepayer.

Our famous old airfield is going to become a nerve centre of business and executive flying and a source of pride and profit to its area. Just at the moment it badly needs help in the form of a long-term policy.

Despite his difficulties with the bureaucrats, and the deterioration of the facilities, Jock Maitland remained optimistic. In many ways Biggin Hill was a success. Aircraft movements were steadily increasing: from 86,000 in 1960 to 158,000 in 1970, to 186,000 in 1980. It was a paradise for amateur pilots. Maitland presided over a lively and varied community of flying clubs, businesses, instructors and their pupils, all doing what they loved best. The profits were tiny, but activity blossomed and the airfield survived.

The Biggin Hill Air Fair

The first Air Fair was held over four days, 2nd-5th May 1963. Its purpose, according to the souvenir programme, was 'to encourage more and more people to fly, for business or pleasure, in giant airliners and medium transports, in executive aircraft and in machines of the excellent aero clubs found in all parts of the country.'

Its official name was 'The 1st International Air Travel Fair', and the biggest attraction was a Vickers Viscount airliner. Long queues formed to walk through the cabin for a glimpse of this exotic form of travel, which was still an undreamed-of luxury for most British people. The 48-page programme was packed with advertisements for tours to foreign places — including the Soviet Union, the Holy Land and South Africa.

There were articles on the history of air travel and the joys of light aviation, as well as thoughts on the glittering future of independent airlines by Freddie Laker, a pioneer in the field.

Among the 117 exhibitors at the Fair were Ghana Airways, Airfix Models, the Jersey Tourism Committee, Hertz Rent-a-Car System, Finnair, Sabena, Pakistan International Airways, the Army Air Corps, the Royal Navy, Decca Navigator Co Ltd., British European Airways, Westland Helicopters, the Park Lane Pen Co, the Westerham Press and Maitland Drewery Airlines. Tombola Prizes offered by the exhibitors ranged from a pair of return tickets to New York via Iceland to the less glamorous but still desirable 'two Car Safety Belts'. They also included plastic travel wallets from Aerolineas Argentinas, a Brownie Reflex 20 camera from Kodak, and '2,000 cigarettes in parcels of 100' from Peter Stuyvesant.[2]

Pleasure flights were offered, but there was no plan for a full-scale air display. Jock Maitland could not resist public requests for a show, however, and a series of demonstrations and flypasts was improvised. Although Jock regarded the result as a 'total pig's ear', an idea was born which would soon grow into a highly popular event. Over the winter Jock approached the Secretary of the Royal Aero Club, Simon Ames, and asked him to organise a display the following year.

Ames, a 28 year-old former Fleet Air Arm pilot, replied, 'I've never run a flying display in my life. I've absolutely no idea.'

Jock said, 'No, I think you have actually, so I'm going to trust you. Will you take it on?' His intuition was correct. Ames ran the air display for the next 47 years. The Biggin Hill International Air Fair gathered an enormous following. The Royal Air Force display

team, the Red Arrows, gave their first UK display there in 1965, and were an annual
fixture thereafter. Each year brought a parade of exciting aerial acts, with a mixture
of daring aerobatics, wing-walking, new and historic military aircraft, airliners, model
aeroplanes, helicopters, skydiving teams and war simulations.

On the ground stood an array of aircraft, military vehicles and classic cars, with a
fairground, food vans, recruiting stands for the armed forces, stalls selling flying kit and
souvenirs, and a radio station. For many years the *London Evening News* sponsored the
event, and its press coverage brought in vast crowds. LBC Radio took over this role in
later years, their presenters Jonathan Richards and Michael Traboulsi conducting interviews with test pilots, fighter aces and other famous aviation figures during three full
days of coverage. Anniversaries were marked with specially-themed shows: 50 years
since the Battle of Britain in 1990, 100 years of powered flight in 2003, 90 years of the
RAF in 2008. Around London and the Home Counties the Biggin Hill air show became
one of the most popular family events of the year.

As well as the Red Arrows, the RAF liked to demonstrate their latest fighter aircraft.
In 1965 this was an English Electric Lightning, which roared unexpectedly across the
airfield at 300 feet, deafening and thrilling the crowd below with the thunder of its jets.
The man who flew it, Michael Graydon, writes: 'I remember that display — the weather
was great and it worked well, although on my first tight wingover I recall being misled
on the height of the ground due to looking into the valley under high 'g' and suddenly
realising why it was called Biggin HILL! A pretty tight pull through was required.'[3]

Another senior RAF officer, John Allison, specialised in flying historic aeroplanes. A

pilot for the RAF's Battle of Britain Memorial Flight (1978–9) and later for the Shuttle-worth Collection (2000–12), he flew one of a pair of Spitfires alongside Concorde at the Biggin Hill Air Fair on 18th May 1986. His collection of types flown includes a Chance Vought Corsair — the famous American carrier-borne fighter — which had not been seen flying in Britain since the Second World War. He displayed this at Biggin Hill in 1983, 1985 and 1986.[4]

Display flying is an art, says Allison, not to be done for an adrenaline rush, or for the admiration of a crowd, but for the pleasure and interest of flying a great aeroplane. 'You're not trying to impress the crowd with manoeuvres, as you would in a Pitts or a Zlin. You're trying to do something that is flowing and graceful, elegant and effortless, something the cameras will love. And always with well rehearsed moves.'

Pilots of these warbirds were often unpaid. The owner or operator of the aircraft received a fee, which offset a tiny part of the annual costs. 'For me it was an off-duty recreational activity, like playing golf. I couldn't afford to buy a spare tail-wheel for one of those aeroplanes, but being allowed to fly it, take it all over Europe, turn it upside down in front of crowds! It was wonderful.'

John Allison is modest about his 34 years as a display pilot. 'I must have been rea-sonably good at it as I managed not to kill myself and lots of people wanted me to fly their aircraft.' The line about not killing himself is heartfelt. Even though all accidents are thoroughly investigated and lead to improved safety regulations, flying at airshows remains a risky occupation. Biggin Hill Air Fair has had its share of tragedies: a collision between a helicopter and a Tiger Moth in 1977, a Douglas A-26 Invader that fell to earth

left
Visitors queueing at the Biggin Hill Air Fair for a look inside an airliner. Ted Drewery and Jock Maitland were keen to promote air travel and package holidays.

right
The Red Arrows at Biggin Hill, 1965 — their first public display in Britain.

AIR FAIR

No 19568

Is this your **LUCKY NUMBER?**

BIGGIN HILL MAY 11-14 1967 **PROGRAMME 2 6**

THERE'S MORE TO THIS JETLINER THAN MEETS THE EYE–IT'S EASY ON THE EARS   BOAC **VC10**

BIGGIN HILL
INTERNATIONAL
AIR FAIR

15-16 JUNE 1991

Shell

OFFICIAL
PROGRAMME **£3.50**

WIN A SUPERSONIC EXPERIENCE WITH GOODWOOD **CONCORDE**

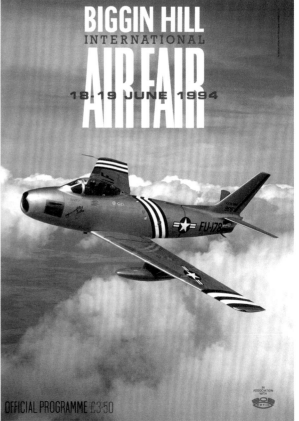

BIGGIN HILL
INTERNATIONAL
AIR FAIR

18-19 JUNE 1994

IN ASSOCIATION WITH

OFFICIAL PROGRAMME £3·50

INTERNATIONAL
AIR FAIR
BIGGIN HILL
Sponsored by the Evening News

Presenting
THE ROTHMANS
AEROBATIC TEAM

25p

above
An English Electric Lightning.

opposite
A Chance Vought Corsair owned by Lindsey Walton and flown by John Allison at Biggin Hill Air Fair in 1983, '85 and '86.

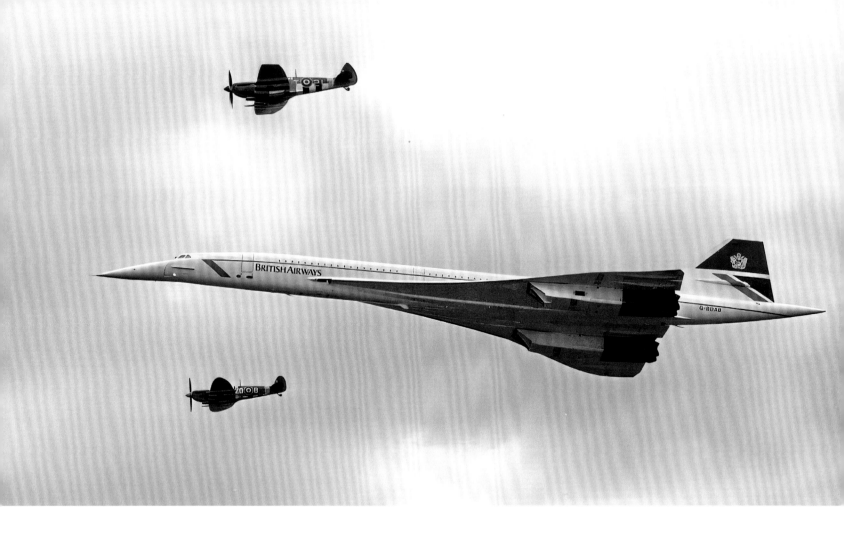

with six passengers on board in 1980, and two fatal crashes in 2001: a De Havilland
Vampire and a P-63 King Cobra. The spectators who witness these accidents are
haunted for years by disturbing memories. Emergency crews and air show staff have
worse to deal with: putting out fires, clearing up the remains, prevention of further
casualties, communicating with bereaved families, and always the press eager for
gruesome details and someone to blame. Fortunately such horrors are rare.

More than half a century of air shows, attended by crowds of up to 80,000 each
day, have brought excitement and inspiration to young and old. Memories, comments
and photographs continue to be shared on websites and forums, paying tribute to
the organisers and pilots who created such a spectacular series of shows: 'Jock Maitland and his team seemed always able to pull something surprising out of the hat...
And many of us — yours truly included — took it all for granted.'[5]

The most famous of all display pilots was the New Zealander Ray Hanna. Starting
as 'Red 3' in the Arrows' first Biggin Hill display in 1965, he was promoted to 'Red 1', team
leader, in 1966. He spent four years in that role — the only pilot ever to do so. Retiring
from the RAF in 1971, he flew big jets for Cathay Pacific until 1981, then with his son
Mark and daughter Sarah he set up The Old Flying Machine Company at Duxford, to
preserve, maintain and exhibit historic aeroplanes for films and air shows worldwide.
Father and son regularly brought Spitfires to Biggin Hill. Ray was legendary for his

daring low-level flights and the disciplined beauty of his aerobatics. A few of his air show performances are visible on YouTube, and there are some particularly fine flying sequences by him in the film *Dark Blue World*.

In 1983 Jim Maitland joined his father's air show business, Air Displays International, which now had a 25-year agreement with the London Borough of Bromley. They organised more than 100 air shows around Britain over 30 years, including Blackpool, Cranfield, Humberside, Sunderland and Folkestone. It was, in Jim's words, 'manic, but incredibly satisfying'.

According to Ben Dunnell, editor of *Aeroplane* magazine, Biggin Hill was always innovative, always setting its own course: 'they had the first ever air travel fair, some great civilian display acts, really interesting war birds, and were particularly good at bringing in foreign military participation. Biggin was one of the last big airfields to have aircraft taking off and landing as part of the show. That included the Red Arrows and the RAF Typhoon. It gave a special sense of a complete airfield-based event.'

The displays were accompanied by expert commentaries from well-known figures: in the early years John Blake and Stratton Richey, later Brendan O'Brien, George Bacon, Andy Pawsey, Jonathan Richards and Ben Dunnell.

Brendan O'Brien learned to fly at Biggin, became an instructor there and flew displays at air shows, including his famous truck-top landing, when he brought his

above
A typically elegant low level pass by Ray Hanna in his Spitfire MH434.

opposite
Jim Maitland

Piper Cub down on a speeding flat-bed trailer. 'It's all about the three 'E's,' he says: 'entertainment, excitement and education.' Doing a commentary means 'massive preparation', studying the aircraft types, meeting the people, making notes, then 10 hours a day on the job, 'giving out emotionally, with zap and enthusiasm. It's hard work!' After decades in the business he retains the deepest respect for the British public — 'particularly their stoicism in the face of bad weather.'

Simon Ames, looking back over 47 years of air shows, writes, 'It was a privilege to see and work with so many talented pilots presenting low level aerobatics in a galaxy of famous aircraft, and to witness military formation teams from the UK, USA, France, Italy and Jordan. What a pleasure it has been!'

His job as Flying Display Director had its own high demands. 'It was a steep learning curve, but I soon learnt to establish the key factors such as getting to know the individual pilots and team leaders, as well as every detail of their expectations — their other commitments that day, height requirement for vertical sequences, timing and runway needs. Preparing a show ran from Version 1 well ahead of the event to anything up to Version 15 by the time all relevant factors had been assessed.'

After the first few years, the Air Fair settled into the rhythm of Saturday and Sunday events, with the flying displays running for at least six hours each day. There were no intervals between acts, which included single aerobatic performances (lasting about nine minutes), aerobatic teams (30 minutes), set-piece ground attack sequences (20 minutes), the Battle of Britain Memorial Flight (20 minutes), parachuting displays (15 minutes), truck top landings (12 minutes), the Tiger Moth Diamond Nine (15 minutes), or a Great War set piece with six aircraft (20 minutes). 'Keeping to time on the day was vitally important as some display items were touring, others such as the Red Arrows had more than one display in a day and had to move onto another show where their entry slot had been fixed and agreed well in advance.'

As with any live show there were tense periods. 'Being in the control tower for six hours without a break and having to observe what was going on in the air, holding discussions with ATC staff on airspace issues, telephoning operational updates to the commentator when there were changes, as well as dealing with phone calls and problems as they arrived - e.g. the engine took time to start, or weather en route prevented arriving on slot — all of this could be stressful.'

Each morning he would conduct a briefing, compulsory for all pilots or team leaders to attend. 'The agenda included a roll call, airfield layout, runway in use, airspace rules, radio frequencies, detailed attention to the published flying display, emergency arrangements; then any questions or concerns, finishing with a synchronising time check.' Clarity on all key issues was the Display Director's prime responsibility, and he insisted on absolute silence as he spoke. The atmosphere, according to one witness, was 'mesmerising'.

BIGGIN HILL
FESTIVAL OF FLIGHT

14TH JUNE 2014

Adult (16+) £15
Child (6-15 yrs) £7
Family (2 x adults 3 x child) £40

Free parking
£2 booking fee will be added to each order

Ticket Line: 01689 300005
www.BHFOF.com
Gates Open 12 noon

London Biggin Hill Airport

Display Seasons

ROYAL AIR FORCE **RED ARROWS**

The 2010 Air Fair.

In his personal list of most memorable days, Simon Ames counts Douglas Bader opening the show in 1966, the United States Air Force Thunderbirds in 1967, the Fleet Air Arm demonstrating low-level refuelling with Sea Vixens in 1970, the 1985 celebration of 40 years of jet aviation featuring the Harrier G3, Hunter, Buccaneer, Meteor, Canberra, F16 and the Red Arrows, the 1990 show with a Sunderland Flying Boat flown by Captain Ken Emmott, and, in 1992, a display by the Russian fighter pilot and cosmonaut Anatoly Kvotchur in a Sukhoi Su27 'Flanker', which won the Hunting trophy for best solo performance. In 1993 the public saw a unique flypast of Second World War multi-engined types, including the Boeing B17G Fortress 'Sally B', the De Havilland Mosquito T3 and the Bristol Blenheim; this was also the first performance of Ray Hanna's Spitfire Formation Team and one of the last displays by an RAF Vulcan bomber. In 2000 another wartime legend, John 'Cat's Eyes' Cunningham, opened the show, at which the USAF's F117A Stealth Fighter made its first appearance and the DH Moth Club's Diamond Nine its last. In 2007 the Battle of Britain Memorial Flight marked its 50th anniversary with a Typhoon and Spitfire formation, and the Great War Display Team took Biggin Hill back to its early days with nine First World War types, including the SE5 and Sopwith Triplane. A French Air Force Mirage 2000 flown by François Rallet won the solo display trophy with an outstanding performance in 2008, and in 2010 (Simon's last show as Display Director) the 70th anniversary of the Battle of Britain was celebrated with a special 40-minute aerial sequence designed by Andy Pawsey. The signature Spitfire display to close the show was brilliantly flown by Nigel Lamb in the character of a Ray Hanna performance.

Jock Maitland started the Air Fair partly as a means of financing the losses at the airport, which worked well when the weather was good, but not so well if it rained and the crowds stayed at home. Credit and debit were always finely balanced. In 1969, with his airport manager Roy Taylor, Maitland started renting out Volkswagen camper vans. Taylor persuaded Phil Johnson, owner of the Wolfe Garage in Westerham, to buy 130 of these vehicles, service and repair them between rentals, and sell them second-hand at the end of the season. The business was named Airport Hire, and it quickly grew into the biggest rental fleet of camper vans in Europe.

Johnson and Maitland became firm friends, and were soon collaborating on a much bigger project, the refuelling of aircraft at Biggin Hill. Johnson was asked to refurbish the old RAF fuel storage tanks at the airfield, which were solidly built but ageing. 'There were six tanks,' he says, 'and I restored two of them. The others we didn't use.' When he heard that Heathrow was switching from tanker lorries to a hydrant system for refuelling aircraft, he went and asked if he could buy the old vehicles. 'These were beautiful tankers, in good condition. They just wanted rid of them. They'd have cost £50,000 new. I got them for £5,000 each.' Johnson and Maitland formed what they called 'a little gang' of four partners to provide the fuel service, although this, like the

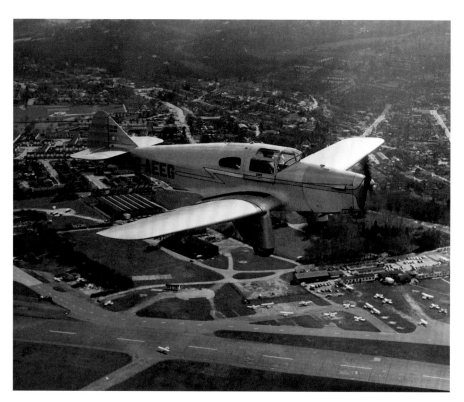

airport generally, turned out less profitable than they hoped because of high infra-structure costs.

Clearly, though, money came second to enthusiasm. Johnson loved flying, and he loved Biggin Hill. His willingness to help, and his practical good sense, were often called upon. He was telephoned in the middle of an air show to rescue a petrol bowser that had broken down on the main runway, with the Red Arrows waiting to take off. Another time he was asked to fill in a large sink-hole that had suddenly appeared on a taxiway. The spirit of improvisation was part of the fun.

Jock Maitland's secretary, Jean Moore, who arrived at Biggin Hill in 1977, says, 'I had no aviation experience, but Jock inspired me. He had such enthusiasm. He was a true gentleman, 100% in favour of his staff. He did everything he could to make work, life and everything around a pleasure and a joy. We all had the utmost respect for him.'

Simon Ames reflects on Jock Maitland's achievement: 'In 2003, forty years on from the creation of the Air Fair series, the Air League awarded Jock the Jeffrey Quill Medal for his lifetime work in promoting air-mindedness in young people. He received the medal from HRH The Duke of Edinburgh at a special ceremony at St James's Palace. Thousands of youngsters have had their first real aviation experience at Biggin Hill airshows. It is widely recognised that this has strongly contributed to recruitment for the Armed Services.' In 2007 Jock Maitland was awarded the MBE in recognition of a lifetime of service to aviation.

Bromley enters the picture

On 2nd April 1974, after 12 years of appraisals and discussions, the London Borough of Bromley purchased the freehold of Biggin Hill Airport from the Ministry of Defence.

left
A 1936 Miles Falcon owned by Philip Mann of Shipping & Airlines flying over Biggin Hill's South Camp in 1977..

above
The Aerodrome Café and other ancillary buildings in 1965, a picture that captures the homely atmosphere of Biggin Hill at the time.

right
Jock Maitland, awarded the MBE in 2007 for a lifetime of service to aviation.

They paid £450,000, undertaking to operate the site as a civil aerodrome for the next 25 years. They appointed an Airport Committee under a Director, John Pooley, and an Estates Manager, Jim Bettridge. Jock Maitland continued to operate the airfield under licence.

At first, Bromley continued the Ministry's unhelpful policy of issuing short leases, but the Council did at least agree to pay for 'any major repairs required to the grass and hard runways, the taxiways and aircraft movement areas.' Another improvement was the formation in 1976 of a local residents' Consultative Committee. This allowed concerns about aircraft noise and other environmental issues to be discussed openly by the community.

Alistair White, who was Bromley's Estates Assistant from 1974 to 1988, remembers 'enormous affection for Biggin Hill' among the Council's officers, and a genuine desire to keep it open as an aerodrome. He organised much of the Council's work on the site and often secured funding. 'I knew how the system worked, how to time your budget bid so it had a good chance of getting through.' Road and runway repairs, fencing, grass cutting, drains, sewerage and woodland management were all funded by this means. 'We also helped out by dealing with the Civil Aviation Authority when they threatened to withdraw the licence. People hated us because we tidied the place up, but in reality Bromley saved the airfield.'

A future role as a business airport was often discussed, and in 1979–80 Alistair White and Bromley's Chief Architect, Bob Matthews, designed and realised a development of the RAF Control Tower, adding a reception area, offices, and aircraft parking.[6] They also built a road at minimal cost by borrowing a Council mechanical digger, excavating a track and filling it with tarmac planings from resurfacing projects elsewhere in the borough. This allowed vehicles to drive around the end of the east-west runway without interfering with aircraft movements. It is now part of Maitland Way.

A report by the Department of Trade, *Airports Policy*, published in February 1978, considered aviation across the whole country. It observed that passenger transport was growing fast at Heathrow and Gatwick, that provincial airports in the north and west were short of business, that general aviation was pretty well served for light aircraft but poorly served for business jets, particularly around London. 'The Government believes that the requirements of business aviation in the South East call for specific recognition', it concluded; 'discussions should take place with the London Borough of Bromley and others concerned with a view to establishing Biggin Hill as the major general aviation airport for the London area.' It acknowledged that Biggin Hill's facilities needed improving, but once that was done 'it would become an integral part of the London airports system. In these circumstances the Borough Council may favour a transfer of ownership to the BAA [British Airports Authority]'. A further suggestion was that 'adequate helicopter facilities should be provided, possibly by the British Airports Authority, to meet demand for helicopter services to and from central London.'

This report endorsed the vision that Maitland and Drewery had been struggling to realise for the past 20 years. The stumbling block, as ever, was funding: huge sums were required for improvements to the airport's facilities. The report proposed that the British Airports Authority should step in with expertise and cash — a suggestion which might have worked if it had been acted on quickly.

Instead there was a change of government. In May 1979, Margaret Thatcher became Prime Minister, determined to revolutionise the entire apparatus of the State. Airports were scheduled for privatisation together with other government properties, services and operations — including water, electricity, gas, telephones, railways, and the London Stock Exchange. In a nation that had become used to a highly planned economy, the sudden sovereignty of 'the free market' meant a revolution in people's thinking. It also meant uncertainty and confusion, but Biggin Hill was to benefit.

In line with official policy, the London Borough of Bromley was required to become more business-minded. In 1981 a new agreement was made, setting up Biggin Hill Airport Limited as a joint venture between Bromley (65%) and Surrey Aviation (35%). According to Jim Maitland (Jock's son) Bromley 'quietly kept the brakes on, but Jock was at last able to work. Bromley started granting 40-year licences. At once new hangars went up. This was the first investment for years. They were happy days for my father. He was on the same side as the Council. It was no longer a battle.'

By now the Airports Act of 1986 had been passed by Parliament, removing the British Airports Authority from state ownership, renaming it BAA plc, and requiring all Council-owned airports with more than £1 million turnover to be privatised so that

The back cover photo from Pink Floyd's fourth album, Ummagumma (1969), taken on a taxiway at Biggin Hill, with road crew Peter Watts and Alan Styles among the equipment. The idea came from Nick Mason, Pink Floyd's drummer, who had seen a picture of an F4 Phantom fighter-bomber with all its weapons displayed. The photo is by Aubrey Powell of Hipgnosis, designers of many famous album covers in the 60s and 70s. Both Nick Mason and David Gilmour, Pink Floyd's guitarist, learned to fly at Biggin Hill, as did Aubrey Powell.

Councils could not use ratepayers' money to finance capital investment or trading losses. The Government was keen to have BAA take over the management of Biggin Hill, and in 1988 BAA, acting through its small airports management company Airports UK Ltd, entered into an Operations Agreement with Bromley Council. The new management undertook 'to operate the airport in order to attract corporate traffic and to provide facilities and navigational aids to meet the reasonable expectations of the targeted operators and their clients', and to 'maximise income to the Council and AUKL, thereby reducing or negating the need for rate fund subsidy from the Council.'

Airports UK were already providing management services at Exeter, Southampton and Southend, but, despite a vigorous marketing campaign for Biggin Hill as 'London's Premier Executive Airport', found it impossible to make it pay. In September 1990, after two years of losing money, and estimating that £5 million of investment was still needed, the managing director of Airports UK wrote a long, courteous but very firm letter to the Leader of Bromley Council stating that it would be impossible to operate as a successful business unless the airport were permitted longer opening hours, some commuter and passenger services, more helicopter flights, and more jet flights — all of which could be granted without exceeding the agreed maximum of 125,000 movements per year or altering the aircraft types already operating there.[9]

previous page
The Red Arrows and Virgin Atlantic's Boeing 747-400 G-VFAB celebrate the airline's 25th birthday with a display at Biggin Hill in 2009.

above
Nigel Lamb, a pilot renowned for his masterly displays, discusses the Spitfire's controls with a colleague, Biggin Hill 2006.

right
Cobby Moore, who has been flying, repairing and restoring aeroplanes at Biggin Hill since the early 1960s. He first worked there with Squadron Leader Bill Webb (1915–2002) in an air charter business.

The Council accepted that 'the airport must be run as a business', but felt obliged to impose restrictions in order to balance profit and environmental protection. Airports UK believed that these restrictions would lead to further financial loss and resigned from the management agreement. In 1992 Bromley advertised for a new operator. In a letter to interested parties Adrian Stungo, Bromley's Director of Land and Services, wrote: 'The Council would like to hear from suitably experienced and qualified organisations who would be interested in putting forward proposals for the airport's future.' They received a bid from Andrew Walters of Regional Airports Ltd, interviewed him, and turned him down. A year later, having tried but failed to put together a new bid acceptable to the Ministry of Transport, Bromley Council placed the airport back on the market. Regional Airports made a second application — this time successful — and in 1994 a new chapter in the life of Biggin Hill began.

1   Letter from ME Tombs, Ministry of Aviation Southern Division, to Jock Maitland, 19 February 1964.
2   This was before the US Surgeon General's report on Smoking and Health published in 1964.
3   Air Chief Marshal Sir Michael Graydon GCB CBE, Chief of the Air Staff 1992–97. Email to the author 5 February 2022.
4   Air Chief Marshal Sir John Allison KCB CBE, Head of Strike Command 1997–9. Quotes from conversations and correspondence with the author, February 2022
5   Quotes are from https://forums.airshows.co.uk/viewtopic.php?t=81291
6   The Council bought the Control Tower with 13 acres of adjoining land for £30,000 on 14th December 1979.
7   Colin Sewell-Rutter to Councillor E.D. Barkway, 21st September 1990.

CHAPTER 6
A NEW LIFE
1994–2022

'He's turned Biggin Hill from a complete shambles into something that is the pride of Britain.' [1]

In 1994 Biggin Hill Airport was far from the brisk, smart, businesslike place it is today. Decaying remains of its days as a fighter station were everywhere to be seen: a pair of rusting wartime hangars, rows of empty brick barracks, a line of old wooden sheds, and two potholed runways blotted with patches of different-coloured filler, much of it loose. 'When a fast jet took off it would blow bits of the runway halfway across Kent,' recalls Peter Mirams, a former Air Traffic Controller.

Peter Greenyer has kept aeroplanes here since 1987. 'The airport had a very, very different feel in those days,' he says. 'There were at least 20 bars, lots of flying clubs and some brilliant instructors, but the airfield as a whole had a feeling of being run down, of past greatness. The military had gone, so it was all civilian, and all private, small, propeller-driven aeroplanes. If you saw a jet, that was something that would make you stop and stare.'

Despite the lack of investment, the airport was busy — at times fantastically busy. Peter Greenyer remembers taxiing out on a Sunday morning and 'being number 20 at the hold, with a long line of little aeroplanes waiting to launch. And the aeroplanes would be going round in the circuit pattern like bees. The controllers were trained to operate huge numbers of them all in the air at the same time, which is something absolutely *verboten* now.'

One of those controllers was Bill Robinson. 'It was absolutely festooned with flying clubs and aeroplanes. A flying circus! Aeroplanes everywhere! It was one of the busiest airports in the UK.' His colleague Peter Mirams says, 'Biggin survived on the stack 'em high, sell 'em cheap principle. The amount of movements was ridiculous. We had no way of recording the numbers: there was a hard runway, a parallel grass runway, a cross runway, and no official air traffic control, just a radio. Often 20 aircraft in the sky, many doing touch and go, which we couldn't count. We were pushing 200,000 movements a year.' Sigurd Reinton, who was often in one of those light aircraft, and came dangerously close one day to a mid-air collision, describes it fondly as 'the Wild West'. [2]

As well as the flying, the schools, the hangars, the maintenance and repair facilities, Biggin Hill offered fuel, paint workshops and charters. Above all it offered fun. The International Air Fair, an annual event since 1963, attracted between 100,000 and 200,000 visitors to its displays, which were some of the most exciting and spectacular in the world. In good years they brought in a profit. Yet the ratepayers of Bromley were losing around £400,000 each year and Airports UK had resigned

from their management agreement because of lack of investment by the Council. They as well as Bromley Council were keen to hand over to someone else. But who would buy such a loss-making venture?

Andrew Walters had served as an Army helicopter pilot — 'the most wonderful five years flying,' as he describes it — and used his experience to start an air courier service, International Messengers Ltd, in 1972. Carrying everything imaginable — bank documents, medical supplies, freed hostages, ship's engines, TV crews — IML grew from a one-man band in London to a global operation with 150 offices in 35 countries. Its Lagos office alone, which began as a wooden shack at the airport with two Nigerian lads in charge, employed 750 staff. In 1986, with computerised tracking of parcels becoming the norm — and huge investment needed to introduce it — Walters decided to sell up. His network, the second biggest courier service in the world, was bought by the American logistics giant UPS for their expansion outside the USA.

Walters felt 'young enough to start again', so he enrolled in the three-month Senior Management Program at Harvard Business School. At a seminar on future business opportunities, three trends were identified: (1) businesses coming out of government ownership, (2) businesses that could save people time, (3) businesses to leverage computer systems.

previous page
A Bombardier Global 6000 landing at Biggin Hill in September 2020.

left
Andrew Walters in 1994, the year his company Regional Airports Ltd bought a 125-year lease on Biggin Hill Airport.

right
Peter Lonergan, Director of the airport from 1994 to 2011.

Walters had worked in aviation all over the world and wondered if it was possible to buy an entire airport. He read the 1986 UK Airports Act, which obliged local authorities to stop putting taxpayers' money into local airports and hand over control to private companies. 'I was the first to notice this. The only airport transaction that had taken place was the privatisation of British Airports Authority (BAA). My concept was entirely fresh in the minds of officials.'

He set up Regional Airports Ltd (RAL) and tried to buy Southampton Airport, but was outbid by BAA. Since they already owned six airports, he complained to the Monopolies and Mergers Commission, who decreed that the sale was legitimate. His next bids were for Luton and East Midlands. The former was withdrawn from sale by Luton Council, and East Midlands was sold to National Express, who were newcomers to the airports industry. 'It was a huge surprise and disappointment.'

Then Biggin Hill and Southend came up for sale. After a few difficulties, he managed to acquire both airports in 1994.

'I was lucky,' he says. 'I had a pal who had just bid successfully on the port of Bristol. Instead of buying the freehold he had taken a long leasehold. I found this was an attractive approach for the two councils that I was dealing with, because they could retain their assets, get rid of the risk, and share the up-side: it was win-win.'

He bought Southend for £1 on 1st April 1994, and on 6th May signed a 125-year lease for Biggin Hill, granting his company, Regional Airports Limited, the right to operate the airport in return for a share of profits or turnover. He paid £1 for the assets and a starting rent of £50,000 per year — a sum which would increase in line with inflation, and more if further businesses were attracted to the site.[3]

'My first big challenge,' he recalls, 'was that I was a sole trader. I was taking over 100 staff at Southend, with the airport losing £1m on a £2m turnover, and 50 staff at Biggin, losing £0.4m on a £1m turnover. But I knew what I was going to do. There was a core of business, and it had been completely run down. The costs were higher than the revenues. I had to cut the costs, do positive marketing, and measure everything. What was the income? How many movements a day? How much electricity was being used? Who was paying rent, who was not? It was as simple as that. My favourite saying is *what gets measured gets managed.*'

The new ownership got off to a good start. The Council helped by assuring all existing customers and residents that there was no change to the previous operating conditions or environmental controls. Within a few months, however, the business was under threat. HM Customs and Immigration, who had provided a presence at Biggin Hill for 33 years, now proposed to withdraw their regular staff and send over officers from Gatwick as required on two hours' notice of any incoming flights.

This was a serious blow. About a third of Biggin Hill's international flights arrived with less than two hours' notice, so many of its 16,000 annual passengers, who included business leaders, celebrities and VIPs, would have to wait for an hour or more for an Immigration officer to arrive — an arrangement which would quickly lead them to use other airports. Three months of negotiation followed, until, with the help of local MPs, an agreement was reached to restore the full service on a shared-cost basis.

To reduce his own workload, Walters asked Serco, a staffing and outsourcing agency, to take on the employees at Southend and Biggin Hill. Serco had been running

above left
Fire crew sweep up pieces of loose tarmac while the Red Arrows wait to take off. Resurfacing the main runway was the first priority for the new management in 1994.

above
The control tower and the first terminal buildings in 1998. The same scene today is shown on pp 174–5.

hospitals and prisons and wanted to expand into airport work. 'They did the job very well,' says Walters. At home in Hampshire, he took on a local businesswoman, Diana Maclean, to help with administration, or as she called it, 'tidying up after him'. 'The atmosphere was electric,' she recalls. 'Can you imagine? Taking over two airports! We set it all up in one little room on the farm. There was very little money around, but Andrew's a wonderful entrepreneur. He had the drive and the leadership to push it through. It was very exciting.'

Serco appointed Peter Lonergan as Airport Director. Lonergan was an aeronautical engineer and business manager whose career included running ground operations for British Airways at Heathrow and a tough spell at the port of Tilbury, where he had been charged with turning a loss-making government-owned institution into a profitable company ready for privatisation. This included the grim task of laying off two-thirds of the work force (1,900 men). He faced the wrath of the Transport and General Workers Union and his car was pelted with stones each day when he arrived for work — a common scene during the Thatcher years. At Biggin Hill, Walters and Lonergan hit it off at once.

Change began with the main runway. Walters had seen the poor state it was in and persuaded Bromley Council to offer a loan of £1.5 million for resurfacing. This was to be repaid out of future development profits. 'Banks wouldn't lend you that kind of money then,' he remembers. 'Not without putting up your family home as collateral, and even then you'd be lucky.'

The resurfacing contract was awarded to Alexander Gibb & Partners and managed by Ben Verrall, who would help with many subsequent projects. The planing of the old runway surface, and the laying of the new with hot tar, was done by night so that the airport could remain open, and continue earning fees, during the day. The whole job took nine months, including the resurfacing of taxiways and aprons, and all the levelling, drainage and landscaping. Not a single flight was lost.

The work was complicated by the fact that a quarter of the runway, 450 metres of it, was built of concrete slabs. To lay tarmac on top of this meant hiring a special new machine from Germany to crack the concrete very finely and make a stable base for the new surface. The result was even better than expected: the advertised lifespan of the new tarmac was 15 years.; after 26 it continued to be in excellent condition.

Managing the airfield at Biggin was full of surprises, says Lonergan. Part of a runway suddenly collapsed and they found three bomb craters from the Second World War filled with rubble and old furniture. On another occasion, they discovered an old Pick-ett-Hamilton fort. This consisted of two cylinders of reinforced concrete, one inside the other, the inner cylinder designed to rise from the ground on a hydraulic lift. Inside it a machine gun was mounted. Two men were supposed to operate the fort, but conditions were very cramped. 'One of the airport staff, OJ, was persuaded to step in and see if it still worked. He found the lever, pulled it, and to everyone's amazement the fort began rising from the ground: 50-year-old technology still in perfect working order! A few moments later we heard cries of alarm. OJ clambered hurriedly out of the cylinder, smothered in black oil. A hydraulic hose had split and sprayed him from head to toe.'

The new runway looked splendid, and had a powerful effect on morale. Walters thought 'We've got a chance, boys!', while Andy Mellers, a young fireman at the time, remembers, 'That was a real "Wow!" moment. We realised then this was a serious company.'

Modernisation proceeded slowly, with a careful eye on costs. 'The resurfaced runway brought confidence,' says Walters. 'and benefits immediately started to flow. But we lived from hand to mouth. We made a profit each year, some years better than others, but always reinvesting in the business.'

Equipment and buildings were bought second-hand. For a de-icing machine, Peter Lonergan drove to Essex with Andy Mellers to buy an old crop-sprayer; it looked antiquated but it did the job. A Land Rover was picked up for £500, together with a truck and a pile of spare tyres. A secondhand Portakabin, its interior skillfully redesigned by Ann Walters, did duty as a passenger terminal building, and a wartime bomb-trolley served for carrying passengers' luggage.

Asked if it might not have been simpler to borrow the cash and do a quick make-over, Walters says, 'That would have been fatal. We all knew that the airport had to stand on its own two feet.'

Every few years a new challenge would appear. The RAF had left Biggin Hill in 1992, and sold their remaining buildings in the West Camp to Jersey-based businessman Dan Graham. Among his plans for the site were a supermarket with a fence across the apron in front of his buildings, which would force aircraft to take longer routes to and from the eastern half of the airport. Walters had to go to court stop him.

In 1996, Dan Graham abandoned his plans and offered to sell West Camp. Walters wanted to buy it, but could not raise the £2 million that Graham was asking. One day at the airport café Walters chanced upon Bernie Ecclestone, the motor racing promoter. Ecclestone was leasing a hangar at Biggin Hill but had been given notice to quit by Bromley Council for storing cars as well as aircraft in the building. He was rumoured to be moving to Gatwick.

'What's going on at West Camp?' he asked.

'It's up for sale,' said Walters.

'Why don't you buy it?'

'Can't afford it.'

'I'll buy it,' said Ecclestone. 'I'll have the bit I want, and you have the bit you want'.

Ecclestone used the West Camp buildings to store his growing collection of cars and to develop Formula 1 Television with live film action of motor racing from on-board cameras — a system invented and tested at Biggin Hill. He moved many of his Formula 1 staff to offices on the site and regularly flew drivers and technical crews to races from there in the company jets, a practice that continued into the 2020s, with plans to enhance the existing facilities. For Biggin Hill this has proved a particularly fertile partnership, building on a long tradition of innovation: an inspiring example of how airports can attract, and reward, high-value modern investment.

In 1999, a serious threat to the airport's survival arose. The London Borough of Bromley had purchased Biggin Hill from the Ministry of Defence for £450,000 in 1974, with an undertaking to keep it open as an airport for 25 years. Those 25 years would soon be up. It was obvious to all that the 500-acre site would make a highly profitable housing estate. Thousands of new homes could be built, worth hundreds of millions of pounds. The only obstacle was the 125-year lease held by Regional Airports, which was now, against all expectations, making a profit. There was no way to break that lease, but life now became harder for RAL -'it felt as if there was a campaign against us.'[4]

This campaign — if such it was — seemed to focus on choking off the airport's sources of income by objecting to (a) new buildings, (b) the noise from jet aircraft,

and (c) the idea of passenger-carrying services. Since the commercial strategy for Biggin Hill Airport was to develop business aviation, which was increasingly jet-powered, together with all the other services it could possibly want, the noise and building restrictions were a powerful threat. The battle over passenger-carrying became so bitter that it ended in the courts of justice.

Headlines announcing that Biggin Hill was planning to become 'a mini-Heathrow' had already appeared in the local press in the 1960s, when nothing more sinister than a private air-taxi service was set up. Even though this was an obvious example of journalistic exaggeration, the idea of using Biggin Hill for passenger services had certainly occurred to Jock Maitland — and to the Council, whose 1985 Borough Plan included the statement that 'The Council will encourage and promote the provision of modest development related to passenger handling, hotel, restaurant and ancillary facilities'.[5]

Andrew Walters had included scheduled services for 20 to 40 passengers and charter services for up to 80 passengers in his business plan presented to Bromley Council in October 1994, which they had accepted without comment.

Even before 1994, Biggin Hill offered a useful alternative for some of the smaller passenger aircraft unable to land at other London airports in foggy weather. 'On one day,' Peter Lonergan recalls, 'with London City under 50 feet of fog, Biggin Hill was in sunshine 600 feet above. We had 74 flights diverted to us.'

Passenger services were running on a modest scale in the 1990s, to Carlisle and Le Touquet (for Channel Tunnel workers and battlefield tours). Requests for other routes were coming in and Walters and Lonergan discussed ways to expand this promising line of business. In December 1998 an extension to the passenger terminal was built and opened by the Minister of Aviation, Glenda Jackson, MP, together with a group of Bromley Councillors.

In 1998 the Council asked for a development plan for the airport. This was duly produced, and it included a proposal for limited passenger services. The Council responded that the lease did not allow such flights. Walters said, 'I had seen some of the Council's reports leading up to the acquisition and letters between the Council's lead officer on airport matters, Adrian Stungo, and the Bromley Residents Federation, in which the Council clearly stated that scheduled services were permitted. Unfortunately Adrian Stungo had since died, so was not available as a witness. Given the importance of the proposed revenue to our investment plans, and despite efforts to resolve the matter with the Council, we felt we had to contest the Council decision.'

The case was heard at the High Court in London in the first week of November 2000. Leases, letters, press statements, planning applications, notes of telephone calls and other documents were examined; witnesses were heard from Biggin Hill Airport, Bromley Council and the local residents' group. After five days, the Judge,

Nicholas Strauss QC, ruled in favour of RAL. The 100-page judgement included this observation: 'The lease contained restrictions ... covering operating hours, permissible aircraft, noise levels and numbers of movements. These, and the length of the runway, would preclude any form of mass holiday traffic. The October/November 1993 memorandum [a Council document] suggests that the "environmental objective" had been "largely achieved", presumably by these restrictions. If so, why should it matter, from an environmental point of view, whether the passengers were travelling for business purposes or whether the movements were of scheduled or private flights?'[6]

The Council decided to appeal. Although ta letter from Adrian Stungo was produced – stating 'there is no restriction on scheduled services in the lease' — the three Appeal Court Judges overturned the High Court's decision.[7]

Walters and Lonergan found this judgement 'incredible' but there was little they could do. Taking the case to a higher court would have been prohibitively expensive. The Appeal Court verdict, as Walters puts it, 'spiked the business. We had been marketing Biggin Hill all round Europe as being open for small passenger flights, and all of a sudden we had to stop.'

After this setback, Walters made a bid for a contract at Northolt, an RAF station in northwest London which was seeking to earn an income by opening up to private jets. This was still, in 2000, a relatively young market in London, dominated by Luton, although RAF Farnborough had recently been privatised and was also chasing business. One Sunday Robert Walters was visiting his parents. 'I was working in marine and aviation insurance at the time,' he recalls, 'and although I enjoyed it and was learning a lot I knew it wasn't the career for me. Over lunch my father said we had won the contract at Northolt. He had no one to run it. Would I like to give it a go?'

The role suited the 24-year-old Robert better than he could have imagined. 'We started with just me and one other looking after two flights a week. Five years later, we dealing with 7,000 flights a year and employing . In that time I learned for myself what customers want, right down to the basics: loading and unloading the aircraft, catering, cleaning – whatever job there was to do, we did it.' He learned to deal with people who 'demand a certain type of attention. They're not prima donnas but they respond to being treated in a respectful and professional way. They come to us to buy time, discretion and convenience.' It was, he concludes, 'a great little business.'

The contract lasted five years. By 2006, however, 'others had cottoned on and big players were bidding'. To compete with them on price meant compromising the quality of the service, and 'we didn't want to play that game.'

By 2006 Robert Walters had shown that he could not only run a service but expand it successfully. His father offered him the post of Business Development Manager at Biggin Hill, reporting to the Airport Director. His brief was simple: 'Find some business. Make it happen.'

This was easier said than done. But Robert's years at Northolt had given him a good foundation and a sound customer base. 'Through good favour I was able to show our customers what Biggin Hill could offer, and start to build new relationships.' He drummed up business by every means possible — contacting principals, family offices, personal assistants, charter brokers, aircraft operators, trip support and flight planning agencies — but the key was face-to-face meetings. 'In each of the last 20 years I have spent six to seven weeks abroad meeting people: USA, the Middle East, Moscow, wherever. We try to go and see as many people as possible. We also get on the phone and find a way to have a relevant introduction, to create interest and engagement. These people don't like to be cold-called or told something they are not interested in, or things they already know. You have to have a good reason to talk. It can take many years.'

The timing of this push for new business was lucky. Looking back now, Robert says, 'The world was waking up, the opportunities were coming thick and fast. We grew very quickly.'

Other areas of the business have grown steadily. The air shows remained popular with the local community, drawing vast crowds and bringing the latest in aviation technology, aerobatic displays, historic and military aircraft, and a host of exhibitors' stalls. These continued every year until 2010, organised by Colin Hitchins, with Simon Ames running the air display as he had since 1964. After 2010 the show ceased to be an annual event, and stopped altogether in 2018. It was replaced in 2021 by a virtual air show run each year by the charity Aerobility, which offers scholarships and support for disabled people who want to learn to fly.[8]

An important source of income at any airport is rental and leasing of hangars. In 2002 planning permission was sought to build a large new hangar next to the terminal at Biggin Hill, to be used by Jet Aviation, a major Swiss firm. It was, says Andrew Walters, 'a big signing for us'. The Council refused consent, however, and continued to block the development for the next three years. Meanwhile Jet Aviation made do with an existing hangar, 446, although 'it was not what they wanted'. Walters went to the High Court again. At the hearing, on one of the hottest days of the year (9th June 2002), he remembers 'it was so hot, the judge took off his wig and said, 'It is by any measure a huge shed, but I see no reason to refuse it.' Consent was granted, but by then Jet Aviation had decided to opt for Basel. 'If they had got the hangar when they needed it,' says Walters, 'they would still be here today.' (The hangar was finally built and is now used for secure aircraft parking.)

In 2003 Jill Johnson, daughter of Jock Maitland's business partner Phil Johnson, suggested offering a special service to clients who wanted to take pets on their travels. This would include checking of export and import documentation, health certificates and care of the animals. No other airports offered this and Peter Lonergan encouraged her

Robert Walters, Commercial
Director of Biggin Hill Airport

to try. 'My first customer wanted to fly to Europe with two Collies in a chartered Piper Navajo. The registration was G-OJIL. If that isn't a good omen, I don't know what is!' SkyPets proved highly successful and was soon copied by other airports around the world. The financial crash of 2007–8 brought an unwelcome interruption to the growing success of Biggin Hill. A housing boom in the USA, founded on so-called 'sub-prime mortgages', suddenly collapsed, destroying banks, building societies, investment and insurance companies and creating panic worldwide. Drastic intervention by governments saved the global financial system, but a recession followed, the worst since the Great Depression of the 1930s. The aviation industry was hard hit, with 30 airlines going bankrupt in 2009, after losses of $9 billion. Looking back on that time, Andrew Walters says, 'It was one of many occasions when you wonder, what next? One minute you think you're on the horse, the next you're on the ground. But we were in good shape; thanks to very prudent management and specialising in a sector with more resilience, we barely missed a step.'

In 2009 demolition began in the South Camp to create a site for a new hangar and flight terminal for a group of Qatari investors. Digging the foundations meant clearing away wartime rubble, cabling, concrete gun platforms and even underground fuel tanks. It also meant the end of the old RAF huts in front of the hangars and other decaying structures. They were never intended as permanent buildings and had reached the end of their useful lives. After the war they had served as offices, stores, aero clubs, flying schools and bars.

One had been the home of the Pilots Pals, the most popular bar on the airfield and, by the time it closed in 2007, the last. Serving good food at modest prices, it had many supporters around the world, as did the calendar published by its owner, Joe Merchant, with girls posing in bikinis, motorcycling leathers or partly unzipped overalls in front of powerful aeroplanes. An alternative site for the Pilots Pals Bar was suggested, but Joe Merchant was in poor health and the business was no longer making money. He took the opportunity to retire to Spain and write his autobiography, *Biggin Hill Airfield: Beyond the Bump*.

Memories of the many colourful characters who have flown and worked at Biggin Hill are kept alive in an Airport Users newsletter compiled by John Willis, who has spent fifty years there as an air traffic controller and flying instructor. Some of the old guard, he says, felt bitter over the closure of the Pilots Pals, and mourned the passing of a golden age: 'I loved it too in the old days. If it was a nice day we would sleep under the wing of the aeroplane, ready to go flying the next morning. It was very, very casual, everybody was a member of every club, whether officially or not, so it was a very social place. And yes, it was great. But you have to be realistic. Biggin Hill as an airport is a huge piece of land. It's inside the M25. There is no way in the world that it would have survived as an airport with light aeroplanes. We couldn't pay enough money to support it. And that's why, in spite of the fact that I don't necessarily agree with everything

John Willis, Air Traffic Controller and Flying Instructor, who has flown at Biggin Hill for over fifty years.

that they do, I think the only reason the airport exists today is Andrew Walters. He had a vision, he wanted it to be a good, successful, commercial airport, and he's invested a great deal of money in achieving that. The fact that he did that means that I'm still flying there — which I would never have been otherwise. It would probably have been a huge housing estate. I live in Biggin Hill and the last thing I would want is another New Addington next to us.'

To most observers the change from a collection of aero clubs on an old RAF base to a commercial business airport was a gradual process. As Peter Greenyer remembers it, 'New staff were employed, security started to change, fences started to go up, gates started to appear, all those things that are part of a modern airport. It was slowly transformed over a number of years. And to be fair a very light hand was employed in managing the old guard; slowly but surely, as they faded away they weren't replaced by people of the same type of thinking. And so the numbers of flying clubs started to dwindle, and if one fell over it wouldn't be picked up.'

In 2010 Walters and his team decided to take their vision into a bigger arena. They were encouraged in this by their planning consultants, Lichfield and Partners, who suggested making a study of Biggin Hill Airport's economic contribution to the community. This showed that Biggin Hill was the second biggest employer in the borough, with opportunities for growth, employment and youth training in the aviation businesses on the site. From this study grew a plan to tell a wider network of neighbours what Biggin Hill could offer. And so LoCATE was born: the London Centre for Aviation, Technology and Enterprise; 'a partnership of public and private sector organisations promoting Biggin Hill Airport as a centre for the aerospace industry in London'.

Local and national politicians were invited to visit and a brochure was printed, telling the world that 'more investment will strengthen the local economy, provide an economic boost to the London Borough of Bromley and play an important role in helping London and the UK to compete effectively in global markets. More importantly, the economic effects will be felt throughout South East London, which has great potential as a place for future growth and investment.'

With the 2012 Olympics on the horizon, this was just the kind of thing the Greater London Authority wanted to hear. The GLA was working hard on ways of improving the metropolis as a 'legacy' of the Games. This was not just about buildings and roads. The new London Plan, begun in 1999, offered a vision of economic development combined with care for the environment and quality of life.

A number of 'hot spots' were designated as Strategic Outer London Development Centres (SOLDCs). The plan was to 'highlight business locations with specialist strengths' . These would 'generate growth significantly above the long-term outer London trend', offering employment and business opportunities in the outer parts of

The North Camp, June 2022. The control tower, terminal building, airport offices and two new hangars, with the City of London on the horizon.

the city, bringing new life to those areas, while reducing the need for long-distance commuting, air pollution and other environmental damage. Activities included leisure, tourism, arts, culture, sports, media, higher education, industry, green enterprise, retail, office, logistics and transport. This was a vision which could hardly fail to appeal to the London Borough of Bromley. The airport's SOLDC status was announced on 10th September, 2010.

With the designation as a SOLDC, Biggin Hill's positive influence was now officially recognised and integrated into the Council's planning policy.

The London Olympics were just two years away, and an increase in traffic to Biggin Hill seemed likely. The airport applied to the Council for an extension of opening hours and temporary permission for flights with fare-paying passengers. The Council asked what extra revenue they might expect to receive in return. The reply from Andrew Walters is worth quoting at length. It explains the financial position, but also traces the success story of the airport over the past 15 years.

> I have discussed the question you posed about the amount of money likely to be generated for the Council by granting the request for the additional opening hours and admission of some passengers who may have paid for their tickets on the small passenger flights expected to use the airport in 2012 for the Olympics. At this stage it is impossible to be at all meaningful on even the number of flights that may arrive because all of the flights handled are "one off" and, therefore, there is no basis of assessment other than the forecast produced by the Department for Transport which was for an additional 686 flights at Biggin Hill.
>
> The final distribution of flights and passengers will depend entirely on the level of activity at other airports in the London area, security regulations, weather and a host of other matters yet to be decided by others. At this stage everyone is engaged in the planning for the event, making sure that the runway and airspace capacity is in place to accommodate the possible demand – but in no way certain what will happen.
>
> It would therefore be unwise to speculate on matters of revenue and numbers and to be erroneous. However what we can say is that the impact of the Games is likely to be spread quite a lot wider than the two weeks of the Olympics and two weeks of the Paralympics, and that all of the benefits will be picked up in the profit and/or turnover related rent arrangement that the airport pays to the Council and in the additional payments we have proposed to make.
>
> It is also not yet possible to assess the financial benefits that are likely to spread across and into the local community and economy, arising from related work through accommodation, car hire, shops and retailing, catering or the 75 additional short term jobs. I suppose it is not unlike the impact of the big stores and super-markets staying open longer for Christmas shopping.

THE PORT AUTHORITY OF NY & NJ

Teterboro Airport

London Biggin Hill Airport

CONNECT | COMMUNICATE | UNDERSTAND | EVOLVE

www.panynj.gov/airp

t.com

Looking at the bigger picture, our assessment is that in the financial year 2012 just the rent we pay to the Council is likely to be in the range of £240,000 to £300,000.

However that is only a relatively small part of the total received by the Council and it is important that the other revenues achieved by the regeneration and more efficient use of the airport are considered.

The rateable value in 2010 of the airport and all the companies based on it is £1.67 million, which at the standard UBR rate, together with the Crossrail business supplement, results in a payment to the Council each year of between £700,000 and £750,000. It is worth noting that additional rates payable, such as those by Sapphire House who chose to be located at Biggin Hill because Formula One use the airport extensively, would add a further £200,000/£250,000 a year.

This means that in 2010 the Council will receive between £1.1 and £1.2 million from the airport and directly related companies and activities. It is already a long way from where the airport was in 1994, when it represented a drain of £400,000 a year of rate payers' money and generated little by way of rates.

Signing a new transatlantic aviation initiative. Bill Baroni (left), Deputy Executive Director of the NY Port Authority, and Andrew Walters.

Of course the hope is that the Olympics will showcase Biggin Hill and SE London as a business area for investment and the benefits of this as a legacy of the Games will lead to a further substantial rise in the economic contribution of the airport to the Council and the local community.

I would be surprised if the Council receipts from the airport, airport based companies and adjoining land uses were not much higher in 2012 and could certainly go higher if the Olympic legacy can provide the stimulus needed to bring the vacant land and long time empty buildings of West Camp back into use.

Please let me know if you require any additional information.

Despite this well-argued case, the Council refused the airport's requests.

New staff, new strategies

In 2011, after 17 years as Airport Director, Peter Lonergan retired. Andrew Walters has the highest praise for him. 'He played a huge part in this business, a delightful man, kind and generous. We owe him a huge debt of gratitude.' Lonergan did a phased handover to his successor, Jenny Munro, who had previously worked at Gatwick and Dubai airports. 'She was particularly good on community affairs,' says Walters. 'Peter Lonergan had always had bruising encounters with the Council, and Jenny worked successfully on bridging the gap.'

In 2012 the Government established an independent Airport Commission under Sir Howard Davies, with a brief to find a solution to London's airport capacity problems which had perplexed governments for over 50 years. Andrew and Robert Walters saw an opportunity to be included in the national strategy and set up a number of research initiatives. One was a visit to New York, where they learned of the role of 'Reliever Airports' in Federal Aviation Policy. These were designated to provide capacity for business aviation near major cities so as to liberate slots at the big passenger airports and help keep commercial flights running on time. Teterboro in New Jersey was one such, offering congestion-free access to New York city. The visit resulted in the signing of a 'Sister Agreement' between Teterboro and Biggin Hill The UK Airport Commission gave its support, concluding that "this may be the best way to cater for the needs of business users without disrupting the wider airport system." This, for Biggin Hill, was 'a major strategic step forward'.

Another initiative was to commission a second, more detailed report by the planning consultants Lichfield and Partners on the value of Biggin Hill to the local economy. This uncovered some interesting facts: the airport and its businesses supported 980 jobs at an average salary of £70,000 per employee: a total annual output of £68.9 million. Given the right conditions for development, this could plausibly rise to £230 million per year by 2031. The cost of failing to allow this growth was calculated at £1.84 billion.[9]

LoCATE
LONDON CENTRE FOR **AVIATION**
TECHNOLOGY AND **ENTERPRISE**

THE CASE FOR **GROWTH**

FARRELLS

"
London Biggin Hill has emerged as a **leading business in the South East** and is one of the **most important pioneers of the business aviation sector** in the UK... it is proving a **very sound investment** for those choosing to base there

Sadiq Khan, Mayor of London

A third research project was undertaken by the market intelligence company WINGX, assessing the potential of Biggin Hill to attract more Maintenance, Repair and Overhaul (MRO) facilities. Walters wanted to maximise property income from the airport's 500-acre site to offset the seasonality of aviation. The WINGX consultants talked to the senior executives of 12 leading aircraft manufacturers and some of their independent MRO service providers with the aim of exploring their organisational and financial objectives. The survey highlighted the importance of location, primarily in or around big cities, the frequency of transient traffic, the support of airport authorities, the presence of other business aviation activities and suppliers, opening hours, the price of building, and land availability. It also indicated that, like car manufacturers, aircraft manufacturers were seeking to become more 'vertically integrated' — i.e. to continue their relationship with aircraft purchasers after sale, supplying the full range of additional services, upgrades and refurbishment. This was a new development in an industry that had previously relied on independent suppliers. Here was a new perspective: an ideal opportunity for Biggin Hill to use its competitive advantages of available land, its location in London and the business it had already built up. Andrew Walters wrote a new business strategy describing three distinct but related roles:

1. As a gateway to London for visiting aircraft.
2. As a home base for aircraft owners and charter companies.
3. As a location for aircraft manufacturers' regional service centres.

The challenge now was to engage stakeholders, particularly the community, in the management's vision for the airport as a growing industrial centre for aviation rather than simply a place of arrivals and departures. In summer 2014 the airport launched an extensive consultation on its masterplan, with newsletters, website, exhibitions and workshops. The key messages were:

Fewer flights, more local jobs
Limits on flights and noise
Economic growth and expansion
Increased Council revenue.

'In short,' says Walters, 'maximum economic benefit for minimum additional nuisance.'

In 2013, after two years in the job, Jenny Munro left for a new life in the South of France. Relationships with the council and the local community were peaceful, and Walters felt the priority was 'to deliver what the growing business aviation market needed.'

The new director was Will Curtis, a respected figure in the industry who also happened to be a first-class aerobatic pilot. He owned Gold Air International with the brothers David and Ralph Gold (well-known in the world of football and magazine publishing) and had been Chief Executive Officer of the Qatari business aviation company Rizon Group. Appointed Airport Director in October 2013, he set about

raising Biggin Hill's profile, enhancing facilities and developing business aviation. London was now the biggest private jet capital in the world outside the USA, with Biggin Hill in third place behind Luton and Farnborough. 'If we were to attract more businesses and employment,' says Curtis, 'opening hours were the next big challenge.' The airport was open from 7.30 am to 9 pm on weekdays, and 9 am to 8 pm at weekends. 'That's just not enough for modern international business. I knew I would need to change the hours, something Andrew had been trying to do for 20 years and which he viewed, at that time, as practically impossible. If I had one main area of influence over the trajectory of the business, it was over how to go about securing that change. I viewed it as a political matter. Until then it had been viewed as a legal matter.'

To engage with the community, he turned to Colin Hitchins, who suggested speaking directly to residents through a survey across the whole Borough of Bromley. A noise-monitoring and flight-tracking system was set up and a team of canvassers was hired. With the assistance of a public relations firm, Forty Shillings, they presented the airport's case, coupling the proposed extension of hours with a Noise Action Plan: 'we need to make better use of our facilities to secure Biggin Hill's future as a successful, small, business airport that creates well-paid jobs for Bromley residents.' The message was well received: 66% of respondents were in favour of longer hours (6.30 am to 11 pm on weekdays, and 8 am to 10 pm at weekends), while 17% had reservations and 17% were firmly against. Similar figures were reached by an independent opinion poll.

Bromley Council were sceptical, however, and decided to run their own consultation. LBHA re-engaged its canvassers, each armed with an iPad linked to the Council's research platform. This confirmed the earlier result. After two years of negotiation and research the Council in 2016 voted in favour of the change of hours.

This was, says Andy Patsalides, 'an extraordinary thing. I can't think of another airport that's been allowed to do that.' Curtis agrees: 'I have to say, to the eternal credit of Bromley Council, they understood the importance of the airport as a key area for job creation.' For Simon Ames, 'This is a good story about democracy: the Councillors deciding in their wisdom what was going to be best for the London Borough of Bromley.'

Including the surveys, the noise-monitoring and flight-tracking system, the campaign cost almost £1 million. It was another example, says Simon Ames, of Walters 'thinking carefully all the way around a problem, looking at it from every point of view, and doing the right thing in the best way possible. What comes over in the whole of that period is Andrew's absolute determination to win that battle. The leadership he showed was fantastic. The determination, the preparation, the lobbying that he did, the open sessions — that's what won the day. For the noise-monitoring Andrew didn't just say, "OK we'll have some microphones set up at the end of the runway", he engaged a top class professional firm. And that was one of the many reasons he was successful. Bromley Council trusted him. OK, they thought, if you're going to do all that, this is good.'

above
Jenny Munro, Managing Director of London Biggin Hill Airport from 2011 to 2013.

opposite
Will Curtis performs an unusual stunt in a Sukhoi Su-26.

next page
A Dassault Falcon outside Tower Hangar 1, with London's Canary Wharf and Docklands in the backgroun

Following the agreement on operating hours, business and investment grew vigorously. Existing companies expanded, new companies arrived. Over the next five years the number of business jets based at Biggin Hill trebled from 20 to 60, and airport revenues rose from £12m a year to over £24m. At the same time, management continued to focus on a 'good neighbours' policy, giving money to local charities, creating a Community Fund, reaching out to local schools and offering employment opportunities: 'Every aircraft based at Biggin Hill' says Walters, 'creates eight jobs. Every aircraft coming to be serviced provides work for many more over its two or three week stay.'[10]

In 2016 Andy Patsalides, the Head of Airport Marketing, saw a new business opportunity. 'We have a company here, Castle Air, with helicopters and pilots available for work, so we came up with a brand new service, London Heli-Shuttle – just 6 minutes in to London, compared with 45 minutes or more by car. It's been a tremendous success.'

In 2017, the airfield's centenary year, Bombardier, the Canadian aircraft manufacturer, moved its business jet maintenance activity from Amsterdam to Biggin Hill, occupying the recently vacated Rizon Jet hangar. For Andrew Walters this was 'a huge vote of confidence'. As the parent company for several brands of business jets (Lear, Challenger, Global Express) Bombardier was 'an ideal partner for the airport. Its presence could only enhance the appeal of Biggin Hill as a business aviation base'.

At the opening of Bombardier's hangar, HRH Prince Michael of Kent was the guest of honour. Jean-Christophe Gallagher, Bombardier's Vice-President & General Manager, told the assembled visitors: 'We are committed to a long-term relationship with Biggin Hill Airport to develop a world-class aviation hub serving as a catalyst for business aviation growth in the region. We are extremely proud to inaugurate our new facility during the airport's 100-year anniversary celebration.' Since then, Bombardier Corporate Jets has invested a further £63 million: in 2020 they commissioned a new hangar to serve customers in Europe, the Middle East and Africa. The hangar, which can service 14 Global 7500 business jets at the same time, was built by a local firm, Civils, and opened in 2022.

In 2018 the second of the airport's large aircraft-parking hangars was opened and was soon full of customers' aeroplanes. Meanwhile, an important cultural initiative was announced: a Museum dedicated to the history of Biggin Hill. Built next to St George's RAF Chapel of Remembrance, and intended as a means of generating income for the Chapel's preservation, the Museum was set up by Bromley Council and is independent of the airport both financially and organisationally. The Biggin Hill Memorial Museum has collected objects, pictures and personal testimonies of life at the RAF station and in the local community, and created a programme of events for all ages. With its own Nightingale Café (echoing the name of a wartime establishment at the airfield) and a group of expert volunteers ready to answer the most detailed questions, it opened to the public in March 2019.

The Festival of Flight in September 2018 commemorated the Battle of Britain in magnificent style. Brilliant aerobatic displays, fly-pasts by wartime bombers, an exhilarating visit from the Red Arrows (who had given their first public show at Biggin Hill in 1965) — everything culminated in a Messerschmitt 109, a Hurricane and a Spitfire chasing each other at low level over the airfield as 'bombs' exploding on the runway set pulses racing. The crowd was enormous, the nostalgia irresistible. As a lone Spitfire roared across the airfield in the late afternoon sun, rolling and banking to show off its perfect elliptical wings, William Walton's *Crown Imperial* march was played. This was the last of the great Biggin Hill Air Shows, which had been running in one form or another since the 1930s: truly the end of an era.

Public air shows generally were by now an endangered species, after a Hawker Hunter crashed on the A27 at Shoreham in August 2015, killing 11 people. Costs had become prohibitive, and the disruption to the airport's main business — with a ban on arrivals and departures for three days each year, as well as a crowd of 100,000 providing a security headache — was problematic. Construction of a new hangar for Bombardier would also take away the main parking area for the air show.

Despite these arguments, the popularity of this event, and the good feeling it created in the local community, were not forgotten. Plans were soon being made to run smaller-scale events and launch a virtual airshow to renew this opportunity for public understanding and interest.

A new Chief Executive

In March 2019, Will Curtis stepped down, as planned, to pursue his other interests. Looking back on his time at Biggin Hill he says, 'I greatly enjoyed working with Andrew Walters. He is tenacious and makes good decisions and I will always be grateful to him for putting his faith in me.'

'What we needed for the next stage of our growth,' says Andrew Walters, 'was structured rather than entrepreneurial management. And I needed it as much as anyone.' Entrepreneurs can have great ideas, they can see the goal and drive the team towards it, but 'they need a really good nuts and bolts manager to run things.' He set two firms of headhunters onto the task, each to provide a short-list of six candidates. 'Then one of them rang me and said, "There's someone I think you'd be very interested to meet." So I met David Winstanley, and I thought at once he was just the man for the job. I asked Jock Lowe, who has been a Director in our parent company, RAL, for 18 years, one of the most experienced men in the business — former Captain of

above
Will Curtis (Airport Director 2013–18), Heather Kemp (RAF Benevolent Fund) and Peter Monk (Heritage Hangar) at the 75th anniversary of 'the hardest day' of the Battle of Britain.

opposite
Prince Michael of Kent opens the first Bombardier hangar at Biggin Hill, 18 May 2017. On his right are Jean-Christophe Gallagher, Vice-President of Bombardier, and Andrew Walters.

the Concorde fleet, then Chief of Operations at British Airways. He met David, and he agreed.'

David Winstanley already knew something of Biggin Hill. Having joined the Navy at 18, he decided after two years to apply to the RAF and in 1986 passed through the Officers and Aircrew Selection Centre. (His experiences are described in Chapter 5.) He was trained as an Air Traffic Controller, quickly promoted to Squadron Leader, and at Staff College took a Master's Degree in International Defence Studies. In 2006 he retired from the RAF with the rank of Wing Commander. He went on to be Head of Security and later Chief Operating Officer at Birmingham, one of the busiest of Britain's regional airports, handling 12.5 million passengers each year.

'Will Curtis had done a fantastic job: he took the airport from humble growth to really focus on business aviation, which is a distinct sector within the wider aviation industry. But Andrew Walters realised that to unlock the airport's future potential it needed to be more disciplined in the way the internal mechanics of the business ran. He asked me to bring in the discipline you learn as a professional leader from a larger

airport. He asked me to add capacity and capability, in both people and physical infrastructure, to leverage our competitive advantage and attract more businesses to the airport. And he asked me to look after those that work for him. "Care for the people around you." So yes, be a strategic, clear-thinking CEO, but do it in a nice way. Do it in the right way.'

Winstanley's vision of the future is founded on an agile response to change, a commitment to sustainability, and technological innovation — a strong tradition at Biggin Hill. Sustainability is a particular challenge for aviation, but he is keen to point out that the efficiency of airframes and engines is constantly improving, and he looks forward to welcoming fully electric aircraft to Biggin Hill. (Trial flights are scheduled for 2023-4.) Meanwhile the airport is reducing its own carbon emissions (down by 55% between 2019 and 2022), and promoting the use of Sustainable Aviation Fuel (SAF). Business aviation is a growing sector, well placed to embrace new technology. '95% of our business is Europe-based,' he says, 'and short haul flights are good for innovation in sources of power which may be limited in range. We need manufacturers to continue developing sustainable engines; meanwhile our job is to develop infrastructure that maximises innovation and preserves the environment for the future.'

All plans were brutally disrupted by the Covid-19 pandemic. First appearing in Europe in January 2020, the virus wreaked havoc for two years. It caused governments worldwide to shut down all non-essential contact between individuals, close shops, pubs,

left
The South Camp in 2022.

above
The Museum, St George's Chapel and the Gate Guardians in 2022.

previous page
The Royal Air Force Centenary celebration at Biggin Hill, 16th April 2018. A BAe 146 of 32 Squadron, on its 100-day mission to 100 places of historical significance, is welcomed by the Mayor of Bromley, the airport's Managing Director, and a party of local Air Cadets, RAF personnel and veterans.

restaurants, theatres and sports venues, and impose a ban on all but the most necessary travel. Airlines were hit particularly hard. Business aviation was permitted, but suffered a 30% slump, and Biggin Hill's annual flight departures dropped from 8,000 to 7,000.

The Airport remained open, however, and responded quickly to the new challenges, focussing on customer confidence while keeping to the philosophy of 'people before profit'. Its popular Lookout Café was turned into a Covid testing centre for passengers and aircrew, named after a local doctor, Joseph Mansi, who played a heroic role attending the wounded on the night of 30th August 1940.

In March 2021, with world trade starting to pick up again and optimism rekindled by vaccines against Covid-19, a new project was begun: The Landing Hotel. This was financed and built by Biggin Hill Airport at a cost of £10 million, with bar, café, restaurant, gym, conference suite and 54 bedrooms for aircrew, engineers and other visitors. A hotel had first been proposed in the early 1960s by Jock Maitland and Ted Drewery. They saw it as an essential component of any modern airport. It would no doubt have given them great satisfaction to see their dream, first outlined in a plan 60 years ago, realised at last.

To mark the breaking of the first ground, Robert Walters and David Winstanley posed for a photograph in front of a mechanical digger. With the Biggin Hill mascot and a Union Jack teapot on the sofa between them, they clinked cups from the prescribed 'social distance', smiling at the prospect of better days to come.

A year later, at the 2022 Chelsea Flower Show, a garden commissioned by the RAF

below
Views from the South in 1995
(left), and from the East in 2022.
The main runway, on the left of
the 1995 picture, goes across the
2022 picture, just above the centre.

Benevolent Fund attracted keen public and media attention with its giant statue of a fighter pilot scanning the skies, circled by a curving stone blast wall, the flowers and shrubs of an English garden and a scattering of woodland trees. Closer inspection revealed perforated steel plates rusting in the undergrowth like the broken remains of wartime aircraft, and a pathway littered with fragments of brick, tile and stone from demolished houses. With all these echoes of war, the garden was a tribute not only to the Royal Air Force but also to the civilian population of wartime Britain — 'ordinary people in extraordinary times,' as the garden's designer, John Everiss, describes them, 'all involved in one story, to try to protect the nation'.

Financed by Project Giving Back, the garden was moved to a site in front of The Landing Hotel at Biggin Hill in July 2022. It was renamed The Strongest Link Garden and officially opened by Randolph Churchill on 15th September, Battle of Britain Day.

John Everiss and the planting designer, Rossana Porta, conceived the garden as a place of contemplation and recall. The project has a strong personal resonance for John. His father Stan was a navigator in the RAF, whose Stirling bomber was shot down over France in 1943. He evaded capture, was smuggled through France and across the Pyrenees by the Resistance, and returned to England to continue the fight. The statue, which is twice life-size (12 feet / 3.65 metres tall), was modelled on John's son George, dressed in period clothing and wearing his grandfather's watch. It was made from 223 layers of marine-grade stainless steel welded between 8-millimetre spacers. It is a striking and memorable figure, a reminder of the dramas of life and death at Biggin Hill, and a symbol of hope and survival against the odds.

left
The Strongest Link Garden, Chelsea Flower Show 2022.

below left
Randolph Churchill with Wing Commander Colin Bell DFC, former Mosquito pilot, 15th September 2022.

right
Randolph Churchill, great-grandson of Sir Winston Churchill, opens the Strongest Link Garden at Biggin Hill, 15th September 2022.

A Beechcraft King Air about to land
at Biggin Hill, August 2021.

1   Simon Ames on Andrew Walters (private conversation with the author).
2   The flying clubs at Biggin Hill in 1994 were: Air Touring Flying Club, Alouette Flying Club, Anderson Flying School, Civilair Flying Club, Classair, County Flying Club, Experimental Flying Group, Flairavia Flying Club, Maitland Drewery Flying Club, King Air Flying Club, Metropolitan Police Flying Club, QS Aviation, South London Aero Club, Surrey & Kent Flying Club, Vendair Flying Club, Wemair, West Essex Flying Club, 600 Squadron Flying Group. My thanks to John Willis for this list.
3   In the financial year 2021–22 the total paid to Bromley Council in rent and profit share had climbed to £450,000.
4   Andrew Walters in conversation with the author. David Gavin of Lichfield and Partners expressed a similar feeling.
5   Policy BHA 6, Bromley Borough Plan, September 1985, p 87.
6   Biggin Hill Airport Ltd v. LB Bromley, High Court of Justice, Chancery Division, judgement dated 21 November 2000.
7   England and Wales Court of Appeal, Civil Division, 18 October 2002.
8   For details see the Aerobility website — https://www.aerobility.com/armchairairshow
9   London Biggin Hill Airport Ltd, The Economic Value and Potential of LoCATE@Biggin Hill (Nathaniel Lichfield & Partners, June 1012)
10 Current community and educational work is listed on the airport website. It includes the annual Armchair Airshow for Aerobility, careers visits for schools, partnership with the Air Cadets, cash donations to local charities, and a variety of projects in Biggin Hill Village.

CHAPTER 7
THE AIRPORT TODAY

L ondon Biggin Hill airport, seven a.m. The first flight of the day is about to arrive. On the ground, a number of teams are ready: air traffic control, ground crew, handling staff, security, customs and immigration, service teams for the aircraft, and a car or helicopter to take the passengers on to their next destination. Standing by, hoping for a quiet morning, are the Fire and Rescue team.

Once the aeroplane has landed, it approaches the terminal building, where a marshal indicates where to park. Bringing the aircraft to a halt, the pilot closes down the engines and the crew open the door. In less than five minutes formalities have been completed and the passengers are free to start their day.

The aircrew finish the paperwork for the flight. Service teams move in to clean the aircraft and, if it is due to leave again, supply it with fuel, water, food and drinks for its next journey. It may be that the aircraft will be parked for a few days, or go for maintenance or repairs, in which case it will be towed to one of the many engineering hangars.

Nearby, in the airport's offices, some 160 staff are coming in, while another 1200 are arriving for work at the 65 businesses on the airfield. Every day is different; every year brings changes of companies and personnel. This tour of 'the airport today' is a sample snatched from the flow of time — in this case a few days in the summer of 2021.

Air Traffic Control

In a glass-walled room at the top of the old RAF Tower, enjoying wide views across the airfield, sit the Air Traffic Controllers. To reach this room they climb a steel ladder, four feet wide and almost vertical.

The career path is equally steep. Recruits have to be keen, ready to learn the language, rules and mental habits of a rigorous profession. Once recruited, they are carefully led through the stages of competence, from trainee to assistant, to fully qualified controller. Bringing on young locals is an airport policy. 'It's expensive to train your own,' says Bill Robinson, the Senior Controller, 'but that's something the management are keen on. And once they've been trained, they tend to stay. It's a nice place to work.'

The trainees are watched by more experienced colleagues. The atmosphere is calm, quietly disciplined. The commanding position of the control room, high above the airfield, seems to encourage this.

Although each of the two controllers has a computer screen showing the airspace around Biggin Hill, their eyes are mostly on the scene in front of them. Pen and paper are used to take notes, and cards slotted into plastic racks represent approaching and departing flights.

In 2019–20 the volume of traffic averaged 50,000 flights a year, approximately 135 each day. But the flow is irregular and aircraft types vary, from little propeller-driven

previous page
Apprentices under instruction from Head of
Airport Operations Barry Sargeant (left) and
Movement Safety Officer Daniel Stride
(right).

two-seaters to business jets the size of a medium-range airliner. There are Spitfires
too, based at the Heritage Hangar, rattling the windows almost as loudly as the jets.
In spite of the complications of mixing fast and slow aircraft, the controllers enjoy the
variety, and are proud to have historic fighters in their daily schedule, even if these
older aircraft must not be kept waiting on the ground in case they overheat. 'Don't let
her boil!' was a parting instruction from the mechanics to many a novice Spitfire pilot.

Bill Robinson has been coming to Biggin Hill since he was a boy recording aircraft
movements in a logbook on summer afternoons. Later he worked as Assistant Controller, progressing to Flight Information Services Officer (FISO), then Air Traffic Control
Officer (ATCO). His Senior Controller was Grant Dempster, then Peter Mirams. Bill
became Senior Controller in 2006.

Looking back over more than 40 years at the airport, Bill sees the biggest change
in the reduction in light aircraft traffic and the increase in business jets. This has been
most noticeable in the past five years. 'You have to bear in mind that one business jet
pays as much to land here as a whole day's worth of small aeroplanes, so it makes more
financial sense. It's safer too. You can't easily mix fast aircraft with slow. We have a
saying here: I'd rather be bored than scared.'

Fire and Rescue Service

The fire crews at Biggin Hill have always been at the heart of things: marshalling,
guarding, providing electrical power, loading and unloading aircraft, clearing the runway of snow and debris, de-icing, scaring birds, even the odd job in the control tower.
This can come as a surprise to visitors. 'It's not what people expect from an airport,'
says Andrew Mellers, former Head of Fire and Emergency Planning. 'People here go
above and beyond.'

In the fire station, built in 2012, the training and readiness programme never stops.
Mick O'Brien and his Deputy, Chris Thornton, man the station every day, supported by
three watches of ten. They must be prepared to respond to an incident within three
minutes, at any point on the 500-acre site.

left
Air Traffic Control, From front: Richard Gunton, Kyle Munns, Joshua Covington, Craig Alchin.

below
Fire and Rescue 2017. Left to right, back row: Mario Bryson, Peter Reade, Chris Thornton, Mark Burton, Vanessa Miles, Tyrone Gabbadon. Front row: Andy Mellers, Mike Tanner, Mick O'Brien.

Their 'appliances' (what the public still call 'fire engines') are six-wheel-drive 30-ton all-terrain fire-trucks equipped with 'monitors' (water cannon) that can lay a blanket of foam onto a burning aircraft from a safe distance. They carry 10,000 litres of water and 1,200 litres of foam for this purpose. 'There's a triangle of fire — heat, oxygen and fuel. If you starve a fire of any one of these elements the fire will cease. A foam blanket starves it of oxygen. We then go to work on the fuselage to protect it from a wing or engine fire. Meanwhile firefighters are running out hoses and gearing up in breathing apparatus. When the scene is safe outside they can think about opening the doors of the aircraft as quickly as possible to help anyone trapped inside.'

All this takes constant practice: driving at high speed to every part of the airfield, day and night, by every conceivable route; working with a dummy aircraft fuselage to rehearse different scenarios: fire in the undercarriage, in a wing, an engine, the galley, the cockpit, a toilet — even under a passenger seat. This is real fire, fed by gas or LPG, although the seats and fuselage are steel, without the upholstery and plastic of a real aircraft interior. In simulations the cabin is also filled with smoke. 'We are required by the Civil Aviation Authority to undertake realistic fire training.'

All staff attend the International Fire Training Centre at Teesside Airport once every four years. Meanwhile it's the 'on-station training programme'. This includes not just fire but all the other work they undertake around the airport, to keep up their level of competence. 'You do test turn-outs until it becomes second nature.'

left
Customer service staff: left to right, back row: Matt Weaver, Linda Orr, George Day, Sophia King. Front: Joanna Parkins, Isobelle House.

right
Chris Miles, Head of the Ramp team (right) with Aaliyah Thompson (left) and Rohan Sullivan.

Customer Service

The terminal building is home to a 20-strong customer service team. Like the staff of a good hotel, they attend to every possible need of passengers and air crew: booking in aircraft, meeting passengers at the steps of the plane, taking them through immigration, arranging hotels and ground transport, and generally making sure that everyone passes through as quickly and smoothly as possible. Customers may be sports stars, entertainers, Heads of State or business people, also their families, flight crews and pets, or the staff of health agencies, film crews (scenes from *The Da Vinci Code* were shot here) and specialist transport services. Delivery of critical organs for transplant and medical repatriation flights are a daily part of the work, which is varied and intense, with as many as 150 flights a day to and from any point on the planet.

Sally Powell, former Head of Customer Services, says, 'Attention to detail is essential. Also courtesy, willingness and discretion. People ask us which famous people we meet at work but we can't reveal names. We're not even allowed to say anything to our families. People would quickly stop using us. Our clients want to be private.'

Fuel

Fuelling aircraft is a vital part of an airport's service — and income. In 2019 around 20 million litres (20,000 tonnes) of jet fuel were sold at Biggin Hill. A much smaller quantity of 'avgas' for smaller piston-engined aircraft was sold — 600,000 litres. Fifteen years ago, sales were similar for both fuel types — 2.4 million litres. The change clearly reflects the increase in business jet use and the decline of general aviation at Biggin Hill.[1]

The jet fuel, known as Jet A1, is similar to car diesel but with 50% less oil. It is distributed from bowsers, which are loaded from tanks on a site once used by fighter squadrons in the Second World War. Avgas is kept on the east side of the airfield, in a separate installation with self-service pumps.

In 2021 SAF (Sustainable Aviation Fuel) was introduced to Biggin Hill, the first of the London airports to stock it. SAF is a mixture of standard Jet A1 and a more sustainable alternative, made from refined agricultural, household or other waste. Regulations permit as little as 1% SAF to 99% Jet A1, but Biggin Hill offers a 33.5% to 66.5% mix because, as Stephen Elsworthy, Fuel Services Manager, puts it, 'we do not see it as ethical to sell 1% SAF as sustainable fuel'. The sale of SAF is part of the airport's drive to be carbon-neutral by 2029.

Operations

A very early decision by David Winstanley in 2019 was to bring in Bob Graham as Operations Director, responsible for much of the airport's everyday life — Air Traffic Control, Fire and Rescue, Fuel, Customer Service, Safety and Compliance, Security,

Flight Operations and more. Modernising operations and investment in new facilities were part of the next phase of development, and Bob Graham had experience of this at airports all over the world, most recently as Operations Director at Birmingham International Airport. He drew up crisis management and business continuity plans ('how to keep things going in a crisis') as well as a register of the top ten risks, with the aim of 'getting knowledge out of wise heads and into new manuals', so that when problems arose they could be solved calmly and methodically. Such foresight was to pay dividends when the Covid pandemic struck very shortly after his arrival.

Finance

The most invisible — but vital —part of the airport staff is the finance team. They do jobs that many of us prefer to forget about: monthly reporting, cash flow, taxation, project funding, business plans, reconciliation of accounts, leases, chasing of debt... The Financial Controller, Allan Finn, is the longest-serving member of the team. He came to Biggin Hill in 1995 after a life divided between accountancy and square-rigged sailing ships, where he trained young people in seamanship.

In the quarter century since he started, paper records have given way to digital, and the offices, once crammed with filing cabinets and shelves of ring-binders, are now clean and minimally furnished. The data that once filled those shelves is now stored on computer systems which Allan Finn helped to choose and set up.

He looks back on the early years with a kind of awe. 'It was very delicate. We had to be so careful with spending. *"Do we need it?"* was always the watchword. The income was highly seasonal. Lots of flying in summer, very little in winter. April was the low point. Cash flowed out all winter, and before it started to flow back in we had to pay rent to Bromley and our fees to the Civil Aviation Authority. We had to time our payments to the day. It's not so critical now. We have working capital at last.'

The Chief Financial Officer (CFO) is Nigel Masson, who was appointed in 2020. after a career that included worldwide postings with P&O, Maersk and Emirates Airlines.'Biggin Hill reminds me of P&O: a great culture to work in, where they recognise people's value. It's modern and fresh, developing and growing, and the balance sheet is very strong.'

As well as the company finances, Nigel oversees the Technical Services department, which looks after the maintenance of vehicles, buildings, taxiways, grounds, electrics and machinery. He also works with an external contractor to keep the IT systems up to date. Despite the long list of responsibilities he goes about his work calmly and cheerfully.

'We have a balance here. It's about managing all the different aspects. Yes, we have to make money, that's clear, but also we're trying to do the right thing. At our

'Marine One' at Biggin Hill, 31st May 2019, the Sikorsky VH-3D helicopter used by US President Donald Trump on his three-day visit to London. Biggin Hill staff in the photo are Sally Powell and Bill Robinson (centre) and Barry Sargeant (right).

executive meetings, safety is always put first. Then there's compliance, which relates to safety, and the needs of our staff. We kept everybody on full pay during the pandemic. We could have taken drastic action last year by cutting everybody's salary by 15, 20, 30 percent, but then what would have been the damage to the relationships with the staff, with customers and suppliers? How would we have been perceived? I think we've taken a very pragmatic, supportive and complementary position to what's been going on around us. This year we've not put up our fees and charges, because we're trying to help people recover from the pandemic. Time will judge whether we've taken the right approach, but if I look back over the last twelve months I'm extremely comfortable with the decisions we've taken.'

Thinking about the future, Nigel is aware that running an airport is a highly regulated activity; it has therefore had to become increasingly corporate in its management whilst continuing to be essentially a family business.

Human Resources

The staff at Biggin Hill are noticeably courteous, helpful, motivated and efficient. They understand the part they play, feel valued in what they do, and enjoy their work. When asked why there is such a positive atmosphere, some people look back to the 1990s when the business was struggling to survive and everyone pitched in wherever they were needed, playing multiple roles like actors in a small theatre company. Others speak with feeling about the 'family values' of the business — where everyone is known personally, thanked for their efforts, and supported through hard times.

Most of the staff have been employed by bigger companies where they found they were 'just a number', an arrangement which no one seems to like. Many have also worked abroad and picked up wisdom, tolerance and humour from living with different cultures and ways of thinking. All in all it feels like an excellent team, led by example and encouragement at every level.

'I've never felt so comfortable or so valued,' says Sam Johnson, who joined the HR staff in March 2021. Andy Mellers, Head of Airport Maintenance, former Chief of the Fire Service, says, 'Lots of staff have worked here for years, and we all feel the same. We've been on a journey together. We've always watched the pennies and focussed on what we're good at: customer service. The customer comes first. Creating the right impression with the customer and wanting them to come back. We're a family business and we're different.'

It's clear that the team spirit has been there from the early days, but how is it kept alive in a bigger, more formal organisation?

The Head of Human Resources is Natalie Smith, who came to Biggin Hill in 2014, working part time, looking after a staff of 70. She now has three others in her team. Meanwhile the airport staff has grown to over 170.

Human Resources, she explains, means much more than recruitment. It's about the entire life cycle of an employee: personal development and wellbeing, teamwork, shared values, openness to change and new ideas, readiness to tackle problems honestly and constructively.

Two key concepts are 'change' and 'values'. Openness to change was crucial when the airport's opening hours were extended, but it's also a necessary part of adapting to ever more complex safety and security regulations, as well as increasing professional specialisation. Values are at the heart of it all.

Maintenance

Andrew Mellers, Head of Aerodrome Maintenance, first came to Biggin Hill Airport in 1989. He had dreamed since schooldays of going into the fire service. He was also fascinated by aviation. His father served in the RAF during the War, and he grew up near Tangmere in Sussex - another famous Battle of Britain fighter station.

Andrew trained as a fireman, first on-site and then at the Fire Service Training School at Teesside Airport. From the start he was given a variety of jobs: 'I was based in flight operations and doubled as a firefighter. I assisted the staff, compiled flight plans for customers, gave out weather forecasts. If we had an incident we put our flight ops hat down, picked up a fire helmet and off we went. It was fabulous, and it's given me a great insight into what goes on behind the scenes at an airport.'

His memories of Biggin Hill in 1989 are of a very different place. 'There were fewer hangars and the fire service was very small. The total staff, including air traffic control, management, security, fire and operations, was only about 35 people. We now employ 32 people just for the fire service.'

Andy Lovejoy, Maintenance Manager, is also a countryman. He has been at Biggin Hill since 2002. 'I think of it as a farm,' he says, sweeping a hand across the airport's green expanse. 'My main crops are grass, aeroplanes and customers. It's the best job I've ever had. Lovely atmosphere, and people are incredibly welcoming.'

There is a lot to look after on this 'farm'. Trenching, electrics, ducting, air conditioning and heating, welding, plumbing, drainage, ground lighting, line painting, hangars, fencing, decorating, general repairs, sweeping the runway and taxiways, helping and escorting contractors… Every day is different, and plans are often disrupted because of a crisis somewhere. 'We like to play a supporting role with every department, and we do our best to keep everyone happy.'

Jobs come along in every shape and size. The grass that surrounds the runways needs cutting every two weeks in the growing season, and it can't be done by day, so he does it overnight by the light of tractor headlamps. 'It's a very peaceful job,' he says, 'and in spite of all the ghost stories about this place I've never felt spooked in nearly 20 years.'

His favourite small job was a call from the handling crew to help a pilot whose sunglasses had fallen apart: a tiny securing screw was missing, and he was just about to leave for the South of France. Andy found a miniature screwdriver, took a screw from his own sunglasses, and fixed the problem within minutes. 'I like to think of that little screw travelling round the world,' he says.

Commercial

Robert Walters heads the Commercial team, whose job is to develop new business, in the air and on the ground, while looking after existing clients. The range of these is wide, but they all have one thing in common. 'If there's one luxury in this world that everyone would love to buy, it's time. Business aviation buys you time.' Studies have shown that a person travelling for work to meetings in different cities during one day can save around six hours on private rather than commercial flights, by flying direct to local airports and avoiding the queues for security and immigration at the larger centres.

above
An e-shot promoting the airport to customers in the USA, 2022.

below
A Fire Service community day in 2016.

Robert and his team always go to the trade shows, run by the National Business Aviation Association (NBAA). This vast professional organisation, with 11,000 corporate members, holds shows in Las Vegas each October, and Geneva and Shanghai every Spring. Hundreds of companies exhibit their products and services. 'You get the entire supply chain: brokers, operators, owners, manufacturers — the whole ecosystem of business aviation. There will be 70 to 80 aircraft on show in a big static display at the local airport. We go, and we don't stop for three or four days, from breakfast through to late night drinks, meeting as many people as possible.'

The Senior Air Traffic Control Officer Bill Robinson and the Head of Airport Operations Barry Sargeant often attend these shows to answer pilots' and operators' questions. More recently Andy Patsalides, the Head of Marketing, has been bringing his combination of branding and sales expertise. 'We fly the Union Jack, because we want to identify with the great British tradition of impeccable service. We offer customers the opportunity to come to a very convenient full-service airport in London that also happens to have a hangar full of Spitfires. That's a very special attraction.'

The 'hangar full of Spitfires' — also known as the Heritage Hangar — is one of the resident companies that contribute to the range of facilities at Biggin Hill, as well as £3 million of income each year – about a quarter of annual costs. The Head of Estates, Katy Woolcott, looks after these clients, 'making sure everyone is on the correct tenancy terms, and creating the right environment for them to thrive.' This means keeping a close eye on government planning policy and checking that against clients' future needs.

Community and environment

Colin Hitchins is Head of Corporate Social Responsibility. His work includes Community Engagement, Environment (committing to carbon neutral status by 2029), Political Engagement and Special Events, aiming to build trust, open dialogue and co-operation for the benefit of the community as a whole.

'The airport is grateful,' he says, 'for support from our local community. This was crucial in our application to extend the operating hours in 2015. In 2008 a community fund was introduced supporting the annual Summer Festival, Christmas lights and the introduction of defibrillators in the village. In 2015 the Community Grant scheme was introduced. This allowed residents to apply for match funding grants in support of initiatives such as Tatsfield in Bloom, First Aid for primary schools, the Nick Davidson Flying Scholarship, support for Aerobility (a flying charity for the disabled), and the Duke of Edinburgh Scheme in secondary schools. Whilst we need to maintain the security of the airport, people can still visit us at the Lookout Café or take part in our annual charity Sunrise Challenge, an opportunity to run or cycle on our runway and taxiways before we open in mid-summer.'

Working alongside him is is Hannah Gray, who is responsible for leading the Unite to Inspire programme, bringing together the aviation companies based at Biggin Hill to inspire the next generation of pilots, engineers and the many other careers the aviation world has to offer. As Ambassador for Science, Technology, Engineering and Maths (STEM), she visits local schools to give talks about careers at Biggin Hill and the importance of science in aviation. Through initiatives such as Futures Week and Work Experience Week students are able to gain practical work experience in an inspiring high-tech environment where there are real prospects of employment.

Hannah is also Community Manager, running the airport's fund for local projects. Recent examples include planters for the village, painting of the Spitfire Youth Club, and equipment for 'Men in Sheds' (a community allotments scheme).

The political context is encouraging. Both Colin Hitchins and Hannah Gray are Bromley Councillors. Hannah was elected Mayor of Bromley in 2020, and re-elected in 2021 and 2022. She is the Council's Small Business Champion and a keen member of the Bromley Economic Partnership. She and Colin share a positive vision of the airport's role in the life of the community, a role which they believe is well understood and appreciated by Bromley Council.

Julian Benington, an Independent Councillor who lives in Downe village, endorses this view. 'In general,' he says, 'Bromley likes to have a profitable airport as long as it keeps within acceptable limits.' While there are Wards that are more affected by noise than others, there are very few complaints. The airport is careful to reduce noise and stop aircraft wandering off the prescribed flight paths. 'Besides, anyone who buys a house in the area knows they are going to hear aeroplanes.'[2]

Peter Morgan, a Councillor since 2005, finds that there is 'no united vision' among his 60 colleagues, although 'no one envisages another Stansted or Luton.' With huge housing targets for the Borough there is a minority who would prefer to build houses,

left
At the Aerobility Virtual Air Show 2021. Left to right (behind aircraft) Liz McConaghy, Jon Windover, Harvey Matthewson, Sue David; (in front) Mike Ling, two Air Cadets, Neil Tucker, Mike Miller-Smith.

right
Dina Asher-Smith, world champion sprinter, who was born and brought up in Orpington. Her local athletics club, the Blackheath and Bromley Harriers, are sponsored by Biggin hill Airport.

opposite
Hannah Gray, STEM Ambassador in the Bombardier Hanger with local students and teaching staff.

but the majority are happy for the airport to 'expand in a nice way without upsetting residents too much'.[3]

After so many tense and troubled years, the airport's relationship with Bromley Council appears at last to have settled into a peaceful rhythm. This can only bring economic and educational benefits to the whole community.

The Aiport family

In 2022 there were 65 companies operating at Biggin Hill Airport, in numerous sectors: aircraft charters, maintenance, management and sales; car hire; catering, cleaning, computer systems, engineering; filming, flight experiences, flight support; flying clubs and schools; Formula 1 racing; hangarage; painting, completions and interior refitting. (A complete list can be found at the end of the chapter.)

Each of these businesses has its own story, and many of their staff are as long-serving and loyal to Biggin Hill as those who work for the airport itself. The skyline is constantly evolving, as new buildings go up and old ones are demolished. A number of hangars have changed hands several times, seeing businesses, owners and dreams come and go. Their histories could easily fill another book.

The companies described here are just a few examples of the energy, ingenuity, enterprise and love of innovation that continue to animate this historic place.

Bombardier

Bombardier was founded in 1942 by the Canadian inventor Joseph-Armand Bombardier to sell the world's first snowmobiles. Over the next 75 years it diversified into transport, service, and recreation vehicles, including jet-skis, trains, snow ploughs and aeroplanes, absorbing historic firms such as Canadair, Short Brothers, Learjet and de Havilland Canada. In 2019 the company decided to focus exclusively on business aircraft. With headquarters in Montreal, Canada, it has 16,000 employees, with production and engineering sites in 12 countries. A fleet of 5,000 aircraft, including the Challenger, Global and Learjet brands, is in service with a wide variety of owners, from private individuals to governments. Its revenues in 2020 were $6.5 billion, with an order backlog of $10.7 billion.

Bombardier moved its European base from Amsterdam to Biggin Hill in 2017, and a new Super Centre, built here in 2020-22, is one of three in the world, offering sales, spare parts, maintenance and refitting. Its completion and opening were supervised by Paul Thompson, the company's General Manager. Paul Barlow, former Head of Maintenance, explains: 'We do the full package here, full maintenance inspections, pre-buy inspections, entry into service, eight and ten-year inspections, engine changes, full interior refurbs, re-skinning, painting... There's nothing we can't do on the aero-planes at this site. We also offer support across Europe, the Middle East and Africa.'

Next page
Inside the Bombardier
Super Centre.

A tour of the facilities is a futuristic experience. A 'skywalk' above the workshop floor allows visitors to look in on aircraft at various stages of work. Light glitters off every surface. A Global 6000 (14 passengers, 6,000 miles range or non-stop London-Singapore) is being fitted with a redesigned interior and new internet capability. Another stands on jacks, its wheels two feet off the ground, engine cowlings opened like beetle-wings. A mechanic sits under one of its Rolls Royce engines. Around him are work tables, lights, tools, manuals, mobile platforms and crates of spare parts — all set out in order on a spotless white floor.

'If you don't mind taking off your shoes, you're welcome to have a look inside.'

The interior of this aircraft is a vision of space and luxury, especially if all you know is the crammed plastic interiors of commercial airliners. Wide leather seats, gleaming lacquered wood, a smart little galley, a folding double bed in the aft cabin... 'One of these costs £2 million a year to maintain,' says Paul, 'so you've got to have a bit of money. Still, it's the only way to travel!'

Corey Trudgen, Bombardier's General Manager at Biggin Hill from 2018 to 2020, commissioned the design for the new Super Centre hangar, opened in September 2022. 'As a Canadian company, we're very conscious of the ties between Canada and Biggin Hill established in the Second World War. The new building is named Hangar 401, as a tribute to the gallant efforts of 401 Canadian Squadron who were stationed there from 1943 to 1944. We're tripling the size of what we've got today, increasing our head count from 160 to over 300 in the first two years of the new site being operational. We're already the biggest employer on the airfield. The precinct itself — the car parks, apron area, hangar, workshops, and office space — is over 850,000 square feet. The hangar itself is 250,000 square feet.'

There are a few reasons why the company chose Biggin Hill,' says Trudgen. 'Proximity to London was certainly important, but I've got to say the charismatic and open welcome that the Walters family offered was a major selling point in terms of a real long-term partnership being developed. The airport would benefit but then also Bombardier would benefit. In the three years that I was at Biggin Hill the traffic growth of business aircraft, particularly of Bombardier products, was not just because we were there but because of the partnership between the family and Bombardier for long-term success. Obviously they're a business and they have to make a profit, but the relationship I've had with Andrew, Robert, and the CEOs, was a real personal relationship, not so much a contractual one of landlord and tenant. Bombardier was generating additional growth for them and vice versa. We sell high-end products to a high-end customer base, and we provide high quality and safety standards. People are buying a $70 million aircraft from us out of their own pocket, so it's all about personal relationships. Whether they're a supplier or a partner or a customer, we're very big on partnerships being beneficial to both parties.'

Helicopter maintenance at
Castle Air.

Castle Air

The London Heli-Shuttle service — 'Six minutes to Central London' — is provided by
Castle Air. Founded in Cornwall for helicopter charter and sales in 1980, Castle Air are
well known for their TV and film work. In 2012 they bought Hangar 525 at Biggin Hill,
where their fleet grew from one to twenty helicopters over eight years. Now run by
the founder's son-in-law, Ross Bunyard, Castle Air offers sales, maintenance, spares,
management, lease-back and charter services at Biggin Hill. They have an air academy
at Cheltenham and long-term maintenance, painting and 'deep engineering' at their
headquarters in Liskeard. Film work has changed from providing platforms for cameras
(now mounted mainly on drones) to 'feature aircraft' which take part in the action of
the film. Their helicopters have appeared in numerous stunt sequences, notably in
the *Mission Impossible* series and several James Bond films.

Declan Lehane, Operations Manager, explains: 'We work with two aircraft types,
the Agusta 109SP, which is a 6-passenger "Ferrari of the skies", and the 12-passenger
Agusta 139, which comes in a plain "bus" version for ferrying people out to oil rigs for
example, and a VIP version, which is the closest to jet luxury in a helicopter. They're
very reliable, they're used as air ambulances. Every single component, every nut and

A Castle Air helicopter over
the City of London.

bolt, is marked with a time code and changed on a regular basis. They have 4-axis auto-pilot, auto-hover, lots of technical aids to help the pilot fly stress-free and able to concentrate on spatial awareness. They're also fully equipped for instrument flying, so Biggin Hill with its Instrument Landing System makes a great base for them.'

He is particularly proud of the company's employment policy. 'We like to employ young pilots. They learn their trade with us. It takes them three to four years to become highly qualified and experienced. We also bring on young engineers. One of them who's just qualified started here as a stores clerk.'

Declan himself started, he says, as 'an aircraft cleaner and hangar rat. So, you see, there's hope for us all...'

Falcon / EFG

Falcon Flying Group is one of the oldest of the resident companies at Biggin Hill and a remarkable survivor. It was started in 1977 by a young aero-engineer from Tanzania, Amarjit Singh Bamrah, who rented part of a hangar in the East Camp as a repair and maintenance unit. By 2022 Falcon had grown into a diverse aviation business, operated by Amarjit Singh and his two sons, employing 30 engineers, instructors and office staff. As well as the original workshop, it now owns EFG Flying School for private pilots and Falcon Flight Training Academy for professionals, both based at Biggin Hill, with other training sites in Luton, Shoreham and Malaga. Falcon also owns and maintains a fleet of single-engined Piper Warrior aircraft for use by other flying schools. It has a consultancy role too, advising foreign governments and institutions on aviation policy and strategy.

Although Biggin Hill is a more regulated, jet-oriented environment than it was in 1977, Falcon has prospered as a specialist in light and heavy piston aircraft and general aviation. Anoop Singh Bamrah, who runs flight training, explains their success as a matter of offering a thoroughly professional, competitive service, and 'working within the airport's ecosystem': co-operating with management, appreciating the commercial environment and adapting to its restrictions. 'We're also stubborn fighters!' he adds.

Shonu Singh Bamrah, who runs the engineering side with his father, points to their training programmes. 'We train pilots and engineers at the British School of Aviation at Luton Airport, which we bought in 2019 from Monarch Airlines. They go on to work for us or for others, at Biggin Hill and worldwide: Virgin Atlantic, British Airways, Boeing, even the military. We're very proud of them.'

Talking to their father, known to everyone at Biggin Hill as 'Singh', one senses something more. A man of deep religious faith and a calm, charismatic presence, he brings a warmth and enjoyment to his work, a commitment to the family — both his own and the wider aviation community — that is rare and refreshing. When asked, in an interview for *Pilot* magazine, if he might ever have chosen a different career, he

left
Falcon Flying Services engineering hangar: Chief Engineer Ashley Soares (left) with an intern.

below
Shonu, Amarjit and Anoop Singh Bamrah.

replied, 'No, I'd do everything the same. Aviation has such a buzz, you know. And you meet so many wonderful people. There are days when the sun is shining off whirring propellers… just seeing an aeroplane leave the ground is a miracle. I always marvel whenever I see it, even after all these years.'

Formula 1

Bernie Ecclestone began developing Formula 1 TV at Biggin Hill in the early 1990s. Thirty years later, in July 2022, F1's Chief Executive, Stefano Domenicali, described the importance of the site in a letter to Liz Truss, MP. He was pleased, he wrote, to see 'the incredible facilities and businesses that operate there', and that Bromley Council had identified Biggin Hill as a Strategic Outer London Development Centre with strong potential for economic growth in aviation-related businesses and high-tech industry. 'F1 is a major tech employer at the site where our Media and Technology Centre is located, employing over 400 highly skilled engineers, technicians, interns, and apprentices. From the technology centre F1 creates and delivers every live broadcast of our races, via links to our team at the event, for a huge global TV audience. In addition, the centre contains studios to record and create content for use across all our digital platforms and is a facility where our engineers devise and deliver technological solutions such as onboard cameras, data systems and track operations infrastructure that ensure every detail of a Formula 1 race is delivered to the fans live. The facilities at Biggin Hill are a very important strategic part of our wider business and we are investing in the site for the long-term future.'

Plans include a '100% sustainably-fuelled hybrid engine in the next few years with fuel developed in F1 that can be used as a drop-in fuel for road cars – dramatically reducing greenhouse gas emissions earlier without additional costs to car owners'; also to be 'net-zero carbon on and off the track by 2030 and all our events to be sustainable by 2025', 'increasing diversity across the sport with paid scholarships, apprenticeships, and internships for students from under-represented groups', and 'continuing to ensure we attract the most talented people to our sport, including all the teams creating the next generation of highly skilled engineers here in the UK.'

The Heritage Hangar

The Heritage Hangar at Biggin Hill was established in 2011 by Peter Monk. It started with Peter's idea of rebuilding a wrecked Spitfire, and turned into a business when he ran out of space in his garage. By 2022 he was employing 18 engineers and trainees, including his own son, Alex. The team has so far restored 12 Spitfires to pristine flying condition, including a 1943 Mark IX for the Greek Air Force. The two-year process was filmed step by step in a six-part Channel 4 series, *Inside the Spitfire Factory* (September 2020).

below
Peter Monk, founder and
director of The Heritage Hangar,
with his son Alex.

One of the most challenging elements of the process is finding original spare parts. Although new ones can be machined, there is a special value in using originals. The price of these can be high. A memorable sequence in the TV series shows Peter Monk, in search of an original fuel pump and an undercarriage leg, visiting a dealer who has a barn full of authentic spares. The dealer produces them, with the fuel pump in its original cardboard box.

'How much do you want for them?' Peter asks.

'£15,000 each.'

They haggle (off camera) and agree a price which is not disclosed. It is easy to see why a full restoration can cost £3 million.

The Heritage Hangar is also a 'living history' museum, with a changing display of impeccably restored Second World War aircraft: Spitfires, Hawker Hurricanes, and their great rival in the skies, the Messerschmitt 109. There are dozens of other relics too, from rifles to bicycles to vintage aircraft instruments. The resident historian, Robin Brooks, author of *Kent Airfields in the Second World War, Aerodromes in Fighter Command* and many other books, organises visits of veteran pilots to the hangar and records their memories with the film maker Jane Oliver. Several of these moving scenes are shown in the Channel 4 series *Inside the Spitfire Factory*.

Tours of the Heritage Hangar can be arranged for groups, but the most spectacular offering is a flight in a two-seat Spitfire, with an accompanying aircraft to carry family and friends, who, while not actually in the Spitfire, have the advantage of seeing and photographing it at close range in the air. A 30-minute sortie over the Weald of Kent cost £2950 in 2022 (about a month's average full time UK salary), with longer flights available to Beachy Head and the White Cliffs of Dover. Those who have done it speak of it as the treat of a lifetime.

Shipping and Airlines

Walking into the Shipping & Airlines hangar is like stepping back into history — or an unusually well-maintained version of it. It is filled with fine vintage and contemporary propeller aircraft, all in flying condition. Its owner, Peter Greenyer, who first came to Biggin Hill in 1987, bought Shipping & Airlines in 2006. 'We're a seven-day a week operation,' he says. 'We get the customer's aeroplane out for him, we put it to bed when he comes home, and we maintain the aircraft for him as well. So it's ready for him whenever he wants to go, wherever he wants to go. He can phone us and by the time he gets here it'll be sitting on the ramp ready for him to fly. We have two hangars side by side, a total of 100,000 square feet. We've got 35 aeroplanes in there, and ten belong to me — I'm the biggest customer! We have nine historic aeroplanes, three of them from the original collection of Philip Mann (one of the founding members of Shipping & Airlines).'

Peter is a great supporter of Biggin Hill. 'It's changed totally since I first came here, but it had to change, and all credit to RAL for their forward-looking vision and investment. The customers we look after are relatively sophisticated private pilots with relatively sophisticated propeller aircraft. They want to be able to fly in all weathers. This is the only airport near London where they can do that.'

Oriens Aviation

Oriens Aviation, founded by Edwin Brenninkmeyer in 2015, is the UK Sales and Service Centre for two leading European aircraft manufacturers, Pilatus and Tecnam. *Oriens*, which means 'rising' in Latin, is an echo of Edwin's earlier career in venture capital, helping young companies to emerge and grow. A fifth generation member of an old Dutch business family (the founders of C & A), he has always loved aviation. When the opportunity arose to act as agent for Pilatus aircraft in the UK he took it on eagerly.

Pilatus is a Swiss manufacturer of high-quality aeroplanes for business, utility and personal use. Since 1939 Pilatus have produced aircraft for a variety of mission requirements, including short and rough field, military, surveillance, air ambulance and VIP. The PC-12, with a pressurised cabin seating up to nine passengers, a range of 1850 nautical miles, cruising speed of 290 knots, low operating costs, proven reliability and short runway capability, was selected for the Australian Flying Doctor Service in the 1990s, which has been the foundation of its worldwide reputation. In 2014 Pilatus launched the PC-24, 'a unique jet aircraft that can land on unpaved runways, offering the cabin size of a medium jet, the short-field performance of a turboprop and the speed of a light jet'. It can carry 11 passengers, with a range of 2,000 nautical miles and a top cruising speed of 440 knots.

Between 2015 and 2020, Oriens built up its staff and capabilities at Biggin Hill to offer everything a Pilatus owner could need, including maintenance, pilot training and aircraft management. 'That,' says Brenninkmeyer, 'was our five year plan. In 2020 we held a meeting to think about the future. We felt we needed to diversify, if possible into new technology and electrically powered flight. Tecnam was the ideal partner: they're very innovative, always coming up with new ideas. They're currently working on electric aircraft engines with Rolls Royce.'

Tecnam originated in Capua, near Naples, in 1948, when the Pascale brothers, Luigi and Giovanni, assembled their first aero-engine from war surplus materials. Three generations on, the company remains a family business, designing and building technologically advanced aeroplanes for general, business and special missions use. In 2021 there were more than 7,500 Tecnam aircraft operating around the world, with a global network of 65 dealers and 125 service centres.

Edwin has been flying privately from Biggin Hill since 1994. 'I'm passionate about the place,' he says. 'We looked at all the options for where to set up the business. It had to be close to London, a serious airport, with an Instrument Landing System and decent opening hours. We kept coming back to Biggin. The management are ambitious, forward-thinking and really good to work with. They're politically impressive too. They've done a great job selling the airport to the local residents and Bromley Council, helping them to see what a positive influence it can have on the economy of the area.'

Edwin Brenninkmeyer, founder of Oriens Aviation.

1   All aeroplanes were powered by piston engines that ran on petrol until jet and turbo-prop engines were developed in the mid 1940s. These burned diesel or synthetic fuel with greater economy and a lower combustion temperature.
2   Conversation with the author, 14th March 2022.
3   Conversation with the author, 17th March 2022.

Resident Companies in 2023

Aircraft Management
Echelon Air – www.echelonair.com/
Flying Smart – http://www.flyingsmart.aero/
Voluxis – www.voluxis.com/
Zenith Aviation – www.zenithaviation.co.uk/

Car Hire
Lloyds of Bromley – http://www.lloydsofbromley.co.uk/

Catering
air Culinaire Worldwide –https://www.airculinaireworldwide.com

Charters
Castle Air - helicopter charters and sales – https://www.castleair.co.uk
Churchill Aviation – https://churchillaviation.com
Flying Smart – http://www.flyingsmart.aero/
Sovereign Business Jets – https://sovereignbusinessjets.com
Voluxis – https://www.voluxis.com
Zenith Aviation – https://www.zenithaviation.co.uk

Classic and Vintage Aircraft
The Heritage Hangar - https://flyaspitfire.com
Shipping and Airlines - https://shippingandairlines.co.uk

Cleaning
Jetwash Aircraft Cleaning - https://jetwash.aero

Engineering and Maintenance
Aviation Consultancy and Engineering Services (ACE) – http://aceservices-ltd.co.uk
Bombardier - www.businessaircraft.bombardier.com
Castle Air - helicopter specialist - www.castleair.co.uk
Falcon Flying Services – specialist in propeller aircraft – https://falconflyingservices.com
Interflight – specialist in Hawker, Gulfstream 550 and Phenom 300 jets – www.interflight.co.uk/
JETMS Completions - www.jetmscompletions.aero
JMI (Jet Maintenance International) - specialist in Cessna Citation and Dassault Falcon – https://jmi-aero.com/
Oriens Aviation - Specialist in Pilatus, Cirrus and Tecnam aircraft. www.oriensaviation.com
Shipping & Airlines – specialist in vintage and propeller aircraft - https://shippingandairlines.co.uk/
Zenith Aviation – https://www.zenithaviation.co.uk/

Experiences
The Heritage Hangar – https://flyaspitfire.com/
Into the Blue – https://www.intotheblue.co.uk/

Filming Services
Castle Air - www.castleair.co.uk

FBO / Flight Support
Executive Handling - www.bigginhillairport.com
Jetex - www.jetex.com

Flying Schools / Training
EFG Flying School – https://flyefg.co.uk
Echelon Air – www.echelonair.com

Hangarage
Shipping & Airlines – https://shippingandairlines.co.uk

Painting / Interiors / Completions
JETMS Completions [formerly RAS Completions] - www.jetmscompletions.aero

Sales
Bombardier – https://bombardier.com/en
Echelon Air – https://www.echelonair.com
Flying Smart – http://www.flyingsmart.aero/
Jet Agent – https://www.jet-agent.com/
Oriens Aviation - www.oriensaviation.com
Sovereign Business Jets – https://sovereignbusinessjets.com

Systems
Centrik – https://centrik.net

Tool Suppliers
HS Walsh – specialist in parts and tools for jewellers and horologists – https://www.hswalsh.com/

left

8th August 2015. An event to mark the 70th anniversary of 'the hardest day' of the Battle of Britain, with a display of 18 Spitfires and 6 Hurricanes and visiting Second World War veterans: (left to right) Flight Sergeant Ted Molineux, Flight Lieutenant Rodney Scrase DFC, Flight Sergeant Bill Clark, First Officer Mary Ellis ATA, Warrant Officer Maurice Macey, Corporal Bob Morrell.

opposite
above
Ray Hanna and his Spitfire MH434 at the Biggin Hill Air Fair, September 2005.

below
A group of Biggin Hill Air Cadets, 2427 Squadron Air Training Corps, at a presentation ceremony, 15th September 2021.

Stefano Domenicali, Chief Executive Officer of the Formula One Group, waves the chequered flag for the company's retiring BAe 146, September 2022. This aircraft regularly ferried F1 teams between Biggin Hill and race-tracks all over the world.

opposite – top and lower left
Air Charter Expo, a one-day conference and exhibition on the air charter industry held at Biggin Hill on 17th September 2019.

opposite lower right
The SkyPets team face the media on National Dog Day, 26th August 2021.

above top
Andrew and Robert Walters are created Fellows of the Royal Aeronautical Society, 21st December 2022. Between them is David Edwards, Chief Executive Officer of the RAeS, who spoke of their "stewardship of London Biggin Hill Airport, particularly in terms of careers, training and apprentice-ships... and their work representing the entire airport sector".

above below
February 2023 the official handover of the new 56-bed on-airport hotel, The Landing. Steven Thorne-Farrar, General Manager of The Landing, receives the keys from Jason Grimble, Site Manager at Barnes Construction.

Afterword

Andrew Walters, Chairman, London Biggin Hill Airport

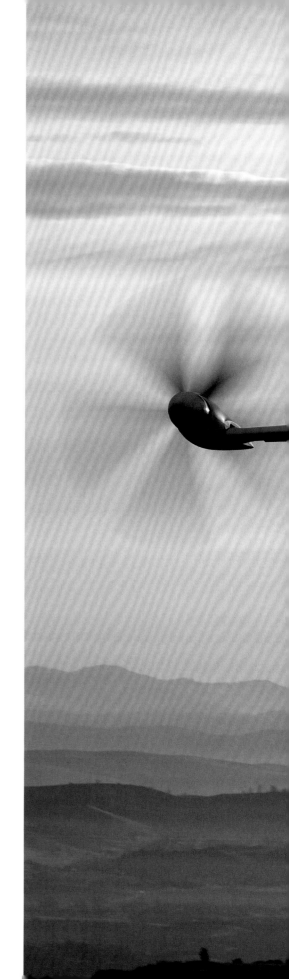

This story captures so much of the excitement, innovation, bravery and dogged perseverance that has characterised all those who have played their part in the nine lives of Biggin Hill. Alex Martin has spent two years in the company of the people who are such an important part of the Biggin Hill story today and who follow on from the thousands who, over time, have made this story possible.

As I write I see our arrivals and departures board with nearly 100 flights today ranging from Rio de Janeiro and Washington to the west and Dubai and Melbourne to the east, with so many others in between and more to north and south, places the famous Spitfires never reached and are now part of the daily connections that this airfield makes possible.

The first chapter of the next 100 years of Biggin Hill will surely relate whether we managed to recruit the hundreds of engineers and technicians required by our new resident companies and the staff to operate the new Landing Hotel in this post-Covid early-retirement phase of employment, whether the economic and energy crisis facing much of the world has changed the demand and role of private jet aviation, whether the new electric and hydrogen ideas for aircraft will have arrived and been a success.

Importantly for residents of Bromley and South-East London, the story will also tell of the closure of the famous Biggin Hill VOR beacon, which has caused millions of air passengers to have unwittingly visited Biggin Hill from above as they circled and frequently descended from 17,000 feet to 9,000 feet as they awaited approval to start the last few miles to land at Heathrow. Such procedures are now replaced by digital systems and better en route air traffic management.

To the residents of Biggin Hill and our surrounding community I extend my heartfelt thanks for their support and encouragement in keeping this famous airfield going and confident that there is just as much ahead in the life of Biggin Hill Airport as there has been so far, and that the airfield will continue to be a leader in aviation, whatever challenges it faces.

An EVTOL (Electric Vertical Take-off and Landing) aircraft built by Joby Aviation in California and first flown in 2019. The propellers can be tilted upwards for hovering, take-off and landing.

Appendix 1: RAF Squadrons at Biggin Hill

From	To	Squadron No.	Aircraft	From	To	Squadron No.	Aircraft
8.2.1918	1.3.1919	141	Bristol Fighter	2.7.1942	8.7.1942	234	Spitfire
17.3.1919	18.1.1922	37 (39)	Snipe	29.7.1942	20.8.1942	307	Spitfire
7.5.1923	12.10.1927	56	Snipe, Grebe, Siskin	3.8.1942	23.9.1942	401	Spitfire
17.9.1932	21.12.1936	23	Bulldog, Hart, Demon	15.8.1942	20.8.1942	222	Spitfire
				16.8.1942	20.8.1942	602	Spitfire
21.9.1932	3.1.1940	32	Siskin, Bulldog, Gauntlet, Hurricane (1938)	26.8.1942	13.9.1942	'2nd'	Spitfire
				18.9.1942	2.11.1942	609	Typhoon
				20.9.1942	28.9.1942	66	Spitfire
22.3.1937	12.11.1939	79	Gauntlet, Hurricane	23.9.1942	20.3.1943	340	Spitfire
2.9.1939	30.12.1939	601	Blenheim	23.9.1942	1.7.1943	611	Spitfire
8.3.1940	2.7.1940	79	Hurricane	8.2.1943	1.3.1943	1	Typhoon
? .3.1940	27.8.1940	32	Hurricane	23.3.1943	15.10.1943	341	Spitfire
10.5.1940	31.8.1940	610	Spitfire	21.5.1943	28.5.1943	41	Spitfire
18.5.1940	23.5.1940	213A	Hurricane	1.7.1943	18.10.1943	485	Spitfire
21.5.1940	20.6.1940	242	Hurricane	13.10.1943	15.4.1944	401	Spitfire
?.6.1940	?.6.1940	56A	Hurricane	13.10.1943	15.4.1944	411	Spitfire
27.5.1940	5.6.1940	229	Hurricane	13.10.1943	15.4.1944	412	Spitfire
9.6.1940	? .6.1940	213	Hurricane	17.10.1944	28.10.1944	91	Spitfire
10.7.1940	21.7.1940	141	Defiant	?.10.1944	22.10.1944	229	Spitfire
17.8.1940	22.8.1940	266	Spitfire	28.10.1944	1.11.1944	345	Spitfire
25.8.1940	8.9.1940	79	Hurricane	29.10.1944	?.12.1944	131	Spitfire
8.9.1940	9.1.1941	92	Spitfire	31.10.1944	30.12.1944	322	Spitfire
12.9.1940	13.10.1940	72	Spitfire	2.11.1944	17.12.1944	340	Spitfire
12.9.1940	25.10.1940	141B	Defiant	16.11.1944	3.3.1945	154	Spitfire, Mustang
13.10.1940	15.10.1940	64	Spitfire	6.11.1944	? 1945	168 (RCAF)	B-17, C-47
13.10.1940	?.2.1941	74	Spitfire	21.8.1945	10.3.1957	600	Spitfire, Meteor
6.11.1940	15.11.1940	421	Spitfire	21.8.1945	10.3.1957	615	Spitfire, Meteor
7.11.1940	24.2.1941	66	Spitfire	29.3.1951	31.1.1958	41	Meteor, Hunter
11.1.1941	14.4.1941	264	Defiant				
24.2.1941	25.9.1941	92	Spitfire				
24.2.1941	26.7.1941	689	Spitfire				
26.7.1941	24.9.1941	72	Spitfire				
24.9.1941	24.11.1941	609	Spitfire				
20.10.1941	20.3.1942	401	Spitfire				
17.11.1941	3.5.1942	124	Spitfire				
20.3.1942	15.7.1942	72	Spitfire				
3.5.1942	23.9.1942	133	Spitfire				
1.7.1942	7.7.1942	19	Spitfire				

Appendix 2: RAF Station Commanders

August 1917 — May 1918 Major HBT Childs	Officer Commanding Wireless Testing Park (later Wireless Experimental Establishment)
April — December 1918 Col. LF Blandy	OC Wireless Experimental Establishment
December 1918 — November 1921 Wg Cdr GP Grenfell DSO	OC Wireless Experimental Establishment
January —June 1918 Major P Babington MC	OC 141 Squadron
June 1918 – June 1920 Major BE Baker DSO	OC 141 Squadron
November 1922 – September 1923 Sqn Ldr IT Lloyd	OC 56 Squadron
September 1923 — August 1925 Sqn Ldr Sir CJQ Brand KBE DSO MC DFC	OC 56 Squadron
August 1925 — September 1926 Sqn Ldr FJ Vincent DFC	OC 56 Squadron
September 1926 — January 1928 Sqn Ldr Elliott-Smith AFC	OC 56 Squadron
[Station closed for rebuilding 1928–32]	
October 1932 — January 1933 Wg Cdr GB Dacre DSO	OC Station
January 1933 — February 1937 Wg Cdr EO Grenfell MC DFC AFC	OC Station
January 1937 — November 1938 Wg Cdr HGW Lock DFC AFC	OC Station

November 1938 — December 1940 Wg Cdr R Grice DFC	OC Station
December 1940 — June 1941 Gp Capt FO Soden DFC	OC Station
June 1941 — July 1942 Gp Capt PR Barwell DFC	OC Station
July — December 1942 Gp Capt JR Hallings-Pott CBE DSO AFC	OC Station
January — October 1943 Gp AG Malan DSO DFC	OC Station
November 1943 — February 1945 Gp Capt HL Maxwell CBE DSO	OC Station
February — April 1945 Wg Cdr GL Raphael DSO DFC	OC Station
April — June 1945 Gp Capt MWS Robinson CBE	OC Station
June — September 1945 Wg Cdr ED Crundall DFC RAF	OC Station
October 1945 — May 1946 Wg Cdr CMH Outram	OC Station
May 1946 — June 1947 Wg Cdr GJ Spence	OC Station
June — December 1947 Sqn Ldr GJ Gray DFC	OC Station
December 1947 — May 1948 Sqn Ldr GD Sise DSO DFC	OC Station
June 1948 — September 1950 Wg Cdr DC Smythe DSO GM	OC Station
September 1950 — January 1952 Wg Cdr AH Donaldson DSO DFC AFC	OC Station

January 1952 — February 1953
Wg Cdr W Pitt-Brown   OC Station

February 1953 — October 1955
Wg Cdr DG Smallwood DSO MBE DFC   OC Station

October 1955 — February 1957
Gp Capt J Barraclough DFC AFC   OC Station

February 1957 — January 1958
Wg Cdr PD Thompson DFC   OC Station

January — March 1958
Sqn Ldr RS Salmon   OC Station

March 1958 — January 1959
Wg Cdr HWG Andrews DFC   OC Station

January — February 1959
Sqn Ldr RS Salmon   OC Station

February — April 1959
Sqn Ldr EF Lapham   OC Station

May — June 1959
Gp Capt GP Seymour-Price DFC   OC Station

July 1959 — February 1962
Gp Capt GN Amison   OC Station

February — April 1962
Gp Capt RB Morison DFC AFC   OC Station

April — November 1962
Sqn Ldr GN Bray   OC Station

November 1962 — November 1964
Wg Cdr RC Everson OBE AFC   OC Station

November 1964 — July 1967
Wg Cdr LF Wolsey   OC Station

October 1967 — March 1970
Wg Cdr IL McCombie   OC Station

March — June 1970
Wg Cdr PE Prior OBE AFC   OC Station

June 1970 — July 1973
Wg Cdr M Scholes MBE DFM   OC Station

July 1973 — February 1976
Wg Cdr R Gebbels   OC Station

February 1976 — September 1977
Wg Cdr KJO Balsillie   OC Station

September 1977 — April 1979
Wg Cdr AL Wright   OC Station

April 1979 — June 1981
Wg Cdr JR Myers   OC Station

June 1981 — August 1984
Wg Cdr FJ Smith   OC Station

August 1984 — November 1986
Wg Cdr DC Boak   OC Station

November 1986 — October 1988
Wg Cdr CIB Skellern BEd   OC Station

December 1988 — March 1991
Wg Cdr ADJ Jones AFC   OC Station

March 1991 — October 1992
Wg Cdr LV Palmer DPhysEd   OC Station

Appendix 3:
Airport Directors
1959–2022

Appendix 4:
Airport Staff – February 2023

1959–90
J.R. (Jock) Maitland OBE

1990–94
Keith Waud

1994–2011
Peter Lonergan

2011–13
Jenny Munro

2013–19
William Curtis

2019–
David Winstanley

Aaran Baggia
Aaron Meayers
Abigail Hirst
Abigail Whitehead
Adam Holmes
Adam Paterson
Adam Crist
Alexandra Taylor
Allan Finn
Amanda Hughes-
    Gage
Ameer Sawyer
Andrew Hughes
Andrew Hogan
Andrew Mellers
Andrew Lovejoy
Andrew Patsalides
Andrew Hill
Andrew Tarry
Annie Holmes
Anthony Embling
Arfaan Pinjara
Barry Sargeant
Beena Sivakumar
Benjamin Burgess
Benjamin Chick
Benjamin Spiers
Brian Darlington
Carlo Cassandro
Catherine Torrance
Catherine Woolcott
Charlotte Fairman
Chloe Reynolds
Christian Huckle
Christopher Miles
Christopher Thornton
Christopher Luton
Christopher Randall
Christopher Higgs
Colin Hitchins
Craig Alchin

Daniel Salako
Daniel Buxton
Daniella Naish
Danziel Trenholm
Darren Smith
David Hewitt
David Linton
David Winstanley
David Harris
David Hart-Bowgen
Deborah Leedham
Dimitri Kontos
Donna Richardson
Duane Thomas
Edward Burns
Ellie Cannadine
Emelia Jones
Erin Marcus
Ethan Syrett
Gary Fowler
George Rogers
George Day
George Martin
Georgia Carey
Georgina Godfree
Georgina Hayes
Hailey Atkinson
Imogen Barry
Isobelle House
Jack Hamblett
Jack Beshaw
Jacqueline Stacey
Jake Haley
James Howard
James Stockwell
James French
Jason Kirby
Jason Stone
Jermain Williams
Jill Johnson
Jill Grimes

Joanna Parkins
Joel Chivers
Jonathan Gribbin
Jonothan Pettit
Josh Sills
Joshua Covington
Kathryn Scott
Kevin Berry
Kian Slater
Kody Wrenn
Kyle Munns
Laura Dimbleby
Lauraine Marsden
Lauren Moore
Lauryn Taylor
Lewis Bird
Lewis Cumming-
    Mendez
Linda Orr
Louis Iveson
Lucy Warburton
Luke Dyer
Macy McKenna
Mario Bryson
Mark Burton
Mark Gee
Martin McCabe
Martin-Lee Harvey
Martyn Harvey
Mary Taylor
Matthew Hall
Matthew Hunt
Matthew Weaver
Matthew Harper
Megan Quinn-
    Edwards
Megan Firth
Melanie Courtney
Michael O'Brien
Michaela Spinks
Michelle Mooney

Mitchell Peter Best
Natalie Smith
Nathan Snelgrove
Neil Hayward
Neil Hodson
Nicholas McCarthy
Nigel Masson
Oliver Woodland
Oliver Isaac
Olivia Deacon
Patrycja Sliwinska
Paul Bridge
Paul Cole
Paul Fitzgerald
Paul Smith
Peter Schwemm
Peter Thompson
Phillip Williams
Punit Wanand
Rhiana Pearce
Rhys Roach-Bartlett
Robert Graham
Robert Allison
Robert Walters
Robert Lewis
Robyn Shaw
Rohan Sullivan
Ruby Masson
Ryen Ansell
Sally Taylor
Sam West
Sam Partridge
Samantha Johnson
Sandor Zsiros
Sarah Bowman
Scarlett Broadway
Scarlett Tournes
    Hardaker
Sebastian Marchant
Shanice-Louise
    Woodman

Sharon Watts
Shenae Reid
Simon Flynn
Sonia Cairns
Sophia King
Stacey Cannon
Stephen Elsworthy
Steven Thorne-Farrar
Tanya Allard
Thomas McGonagle
Thomas Lock
Timothy Martin
Tracey Cross
Vanessa Miles
Veronica Bickley
William Robinson
Zoe Bullas

Acknowledgements

My particular thanks go to Andrew Walters, Chairman of London Biggin Hill Airport, and Simon Ames, former Head of Public Relations and Display Director at the Biggin Hill Air Fair, for inviting me to write this book, and for their tireless help with research.

From the Royal Air Force, I am deeply indebted to Air Chief Marshal Sir Michael Graydon for his incisive Foreword, as well as to Air Chief Marshal Sir John Allison, Air Commodore Graham Pitchfork, Squadron Leader John Hext and his fellow Hunter pilots Malcolm Fraser and Roger Hymans, and Flight Lieutenant Andrew Simpson, who gave their time and knowledge so freely and entertainingly. Having spent several years writing about the Royal Air Force, it has been fascinating to learn more about the process of officer and aircrew selection, which was carried out at Biggin Hill over 30 years with exemplary thoroughness, fairness and humanity. In the course of many conversations I have come to see and feel the continuity of the tradition that began with the Royal Flying Corps in the First World War, achieved such brilliant victories in the Second, and lives on unmistakably today. Everyone in Britain owes these people an enduring debt of honour and respect.

I would also like to express my thanks to the entire staff of London Biggin Hill Airport, whose busy lives I interrupted without mercy, but who always treated me with the greatest kindness. Looking behind the scenes at an airport is a highly educational experience. I will never forget a morning spent on emergency exercises with the Fire Service, who bear their tremendous responsibilities (and drive their huge vehicles) with such admirable spirit, discipline and enthusiasm. A day with Air Traffic Control ran that one a close second; to Bill Robinson and his excellent team I am greatly obliged for their patient explanations of the mysteries of their trade.

I must also mention with gratitude Katie Williams, Director of the Biggin Hill Memorial Museum and the volunteer staff, particularly David Cole, Paul Grant and Geoff Parmakis; Peter Monk and Robin Brooks at the Heritage Hangar; and Jim Maitland, son of the immortal Jock. They have all been immensely helpful, and this book would have been a great deal less colourful without their contributions.

Finally, my heartfelt thanks to the following for sharing photographs, memories and understanding of Biggin Hill past and present: Councillor Julian Benington, Martin Boycott-Brown, Edwin Brenninkmeyer, Amarjit Singh Bamrah and his sons Anoop and Shonu, Mel Courtney, Will Curtis, Les Dickson, Ben Dunnell, Kate Edwards, Stephen Elsworthy, Allan Finn, Georgina Godfree (who took many of the photographs), Bob Graham, Geoff Greensmith, Peter Greenyer, David Griffin, Richard Gunton, Colin Hitchins, Aaron Hughes, Amanda Hughes-Gage, Jill Johnson, Phil Johnson, Declan Lehane, Deborah Leedham, Peter Lonergan, Andy Lovejoy, Jock Lowe, Nigel Masson, Martin McCabe, Andy Mellers, Peter Mirams, Alex Monk, Cobby Moore, Jean Moore, Councillor Peter Morgan, Kyle Munns, John Nelson, Brendan O'Brien, Mick O'Brien, the documentary film-maker Jane Oliver, Peter Osborne, Andy Patsalides, Sally Powell, Sigurd Reinton, Mike Rivett, Norman Rivett, Bill Robinson, Barry Sargeant, Andy Saunders, Kathryn Scott, Natalie Smith, Chris Thornton, Corey Trudgen, Ann Walters, Robert Walters, Chris Webb, Jon Windover, Alistair White, John White (Hunter pilots group), John Willis, David Winstanley and Katy Woolcott.

Although it is not customary to draw attention to a designer's work in such Acknowledgements, I wish to pay special tribute to the design artist behind this book, Misha Anikst. Trained as an architect in Moscow, he moved to London in 1990, and has been creating magnificent books ever since. Every historic photograph has been subtly and beautifully restored by him, while of course the layout of text and pictures, so elegant, natural and appealing to the eye, speaks for itself. This is the fourth book we have done together over 15 years; it has been a privilege and pleasure to work with him.

Alex Martin

Photo Credits

No 2427 (Biggin Hill) Squadron Air Training Corps: 13.
Alamy/2ebill: 134 left; Avpics: 156; Philip Bird: 154-155; Hideo Kurihara: 2-3.
Simon Ames: 134 right; Jock Maitland: 151 right.
Reproduced by kind permission of the Master and Fellows of Balliol College: 19.
Ian Bowskill: 141, 143.
Martin Boycott-Brown Collection: 79.
Bromley Library: 129 right.
Robin Brooks Collection: 24 bottom, 67, 75, 80 right, 84 top, 85.
Castle Air/Lloyd Horgan: 220.
Dave Cole: 82, 107.
Commonwealth War Graves Commission: 70.
Les Dickson: 157, 163, 192.
Oliver Dixon: 196 top.
Richard Geiger: 42.
Getty Images/Evening Standard/Hulton Archive: 137; Dougles Miller: 114 right; Museum of Flight Foundation: 133; Popperfoto: 118.
Air Chief Marshal Sir Michael Graydon: 7.
David Griffin: 104, 116 top.
John Hext: 116 bottom, 117.
© Imperial War Museum: 12 bottom, 25, 33, 36, 54, 58, 59, 62, 63, 64, 72, 76, 77, 78, 80 left, 81 right, 84 bottom, 88, 89, 92, 97, 120.
Courtesy of Joby Aviation. © Joby Aero, Inc.: 241.
LBHA [London Biggin Hill Airport] Collection: 106, 138 left, 138 top right, 138 bottom right, 139, 146 top left, 146 top right, 146 bottom left, 146 bottom right, 147, 149, 162, 166-167, 171, 172, 176, 178, 180-181, 182, 185, 186, 187, 194, 195, 198, 200-201, 204, 207, 209, 214, 232, top, 232 bottom, 236 top, 236 bottom left, 236 bottom right, 237, 238-239; F1: 225; Georgina Godfree: 171, 172, 214 left, 219, 222, 226, 228, 233 bottom, 234-235, 237 bottom, 238-239; Michael Rivett: 174-175, 188-189, 196 bottom, 197.
LBHA Fire Service: 203.
London Borough of Bromley/Matt James: 214 right.
Peter Lonergan: 161.
Jim Maitland: 128 right, 145.
Alex Martin: 18 right, 91, 102-103, 111, 119, 122 top, 122 bottom, 191, 196 bottom, 202, 205.
Mary Evans Picture Library/© aviation-images.com: 28-29; © Hugh W. Cowin Aviation Collection: 16; © Illustrated London News Ltd: 98-99; Keystone Pictures USA: 110.
MOD/Cpl Andy Benson: 126-127.
National Library of Scotland: 10 top.

WH Nelson: 10 bottom, 26 left.
Bob Ogley Collection: 66.
Oriens Aviation: 230.
Adrian Pingstone: 140.
© Pink Floyd Music Ltd 1969: 153.
G.R. Pitchfork Collection: 81 left, 95, 105, 108, 121.
Paul K. Porter, @paulkporter: 193, 216-217.
RAF Museum: 12 top, 17 bottom, 20, 26 right, 27, 30 bottom, 49, 60, 61; Copyright Charles Brown Collection: 44, 109.
Michael Rivett: 148-149, 190, 212, 233 top.
Norman Rivett: 130, 131, 132, 135, 136, 150 left, 150 right.
San Diego Air and Space Museum Archive; 37.
Andy Saunders Collection: 52-53, 96, 101, 115.
Don Shearman: 35.
Shipping & Airlines: 229.
Shutterstock/Paul Drabot: 144; Ronald Fortune/ANL: 129 left.
Anoop Singh Bamrah: 223.
A Thomas via Robin Brooks: 83 right.
TopFoto: 128 left; John Topham: 48.
Walters Family: 160.
John Wendover: 183.
John Willis: 172.

Printed Sources

Biggin Hill Festival of Flight printed programmes.

Paul Brickhill, *Reach for the Sky*
Inspiring biography of Douglas Bader written by a fellow pilot .

Robin J. Brooks, *Kent Airfields in the Second World War*
A useful and thorough book written by the resident historian at Biggin Hill's Heritage Hangar, who has also written a guide to all the wartime airfields of Britain.

Russell W Burns, *Communications, An International History of the Formative Years* (I.E.E., 2003)
Much useful material from a specialised area.

Pierre Clostermann, *The Big Show (Le Grand Cirque)*
A vivid account of a fighter pilot's life in one of the Free French squadrons at Biggin Hill during the Second World War.

Alan Deere, *Nine Lives*
A New Zealand fighter pilot's story, very well told.

Douglas C. Dildy, *Battle of Britain 1940: The Luftwaffe's 'Eagle Attack'*
Good maps/diagrams, plus German archive material .

Paul Gallico, *The Hurricane Story*
A passionate homage to a great airplane. 'She was loved and trusted by every man whoever knew her. She was unique in the heavens.'

Stuart Hadaway, *The British Airman of the Second World War*
Interesting on the practical, physical details of life.

Richard Hillary, *The Last Enemy*
Still a thrilling read. Written during WW2 by a young fighter pilot. Includes much about recovering from burns in the care of Archibald Macindoe at East Grinstead.

John James, *The Paladins. A social history of the RAF up to the outbreak of the Second World War*
Sharp, often cynical account from an insider who still manages to convey his admiration for the work of Trenchard, Dowding and others.

Johnny Kent, *One of the Few*
A Canadian fighter pilot's memoir, vivid and moving. Kent led a Polish squadron before taking over 92 Squadron at Biggin Hill.

Brian Kingcome, *A Willingness to Die, Memories From Fighter Command*
Breezy but deeply thoughtful and impressive memoir by a fighter pilot who served at Biggin Hill in the Second World War.

Arthur Lee, *No Parachute*
Detailed and lively diary of a fighter pilot in France during the First World War. A number of Lee's companions also served at Biggin Hill.

Joshua Levine, *Forgotten Voices of the Blitz and the Battle for Britain*
Skilfully assembled anthology of eyewitness accounts.

Cecil Lewis, *Sagittarius Rising*
A classic pilot's memoir of the First World War.

Joseph Merchant, *Biggin Hill Airfield, Beyond the Bump* Life at Biggin Hill in the civilian years.

Tom Neil, *Gun Button to Fire*
Memoirs of a fighter pilot who did not serve at Biggin Hill, of interest for comparison and for his frank descriptions of the frustrations and difficulties of the pilot's life.

John Nelson, *Grandfather's Biggin Hill*
Work by the local photographer W.H. Nelson who recorded life in and around the village 1900–26. The book was edited and published by his grandson John Nelson. The first edition is hard to find, but a second edition, published by Bromley Library, is still available.

Bob Ogley, *Biggin on the Bump*
Useful source of pictures, stories, characters and lists (eg list of squadrons stationed at BH)

Bob Ogley, *Ghosts of Biggin Hill*
Some intriguing ghost stories here, but most of the book is a thoughtful and informative account of service personnel and civilians who died at Biggin Hill in wartime.

Peter Osborne, *RAF Biggin Hill, The Other Side Of The Bump*
  Thorough and well-illustrated account of experimental work
  on radio communication and sound location at Biggin Hill
  from the First to the Second World War.

Hardit Malik Singh, *A Little Work, A Little Play*
  The autobiography of the 'flying Sikh', a First World War fighter
  pilot stationed at Biggin Hill in 1918. Unusual and fascinating in
  every way.

Jon E.C. Tan, *Aces, Airmen and the Biggin Hill Wing: A Collective Memoir
  1941 – 1942*
  A pioneering book that uses the personal papers of the
  author's grandfather and other sources to explore the lives of
  armourers at Biggin Hill in 1941-2. Shines light on some of the
  least-known aspects of RAF history.

Daniel Todman, *Britain's War (Vol 1, 1937–41)*
  A scholarly, wide-ranging yet readable book which looks hard
  (sometimes painfully hard) at some of the myths of the Second
  World War. Contains memorable eye-witness accounts,
  including scenes of chaos in the Blitz.

Graham Wallace, *RAF Biggin Hill* (1957)
  Methodical, lively, well-written narrative history, WW1
  through to the end of WW2. Lots of very good technical detail,
  anecdotes, history of the site etc.

Geoffrey Wellum, *First Light*.
  A Spitfire pilot's story, written fifty years after the Second
  World War. A vivid, thoughtful book that fills in much of the
  emotional and physical detail that was left out of accounts
  written at the time. Chapter 4 is particularly good on the daily
  life of a fighter pilot at Biggin Hill in 1940.

Nick Wright, *The Bump*
  Accurate and lively, but brief.

Internet
https://bigginhillairport.com

http://bigginhill.co.uk/hst_intro.htm

http://www.bigginhill-history.co.uk/

https://www.iwm.org.uk/

https://collections.rafmuseum.org.uk/

Allison Marsh, 'In World War I, British Pilots Had Wireless Phones in
  the Cockpit' (https://spectrum.ieee.org/in-world-war-i-british-
  biplanes-had-wireless-phones-in-cockpit)
*Note: This does not mention Biggin Hill and gives all the credit to the
  Marconi company.*

Archives and Libraries
Bromley Central Library

Imperial War Museum (with many interviews and photographs
  available online)

The National Archives

Regional Airports Ltd office records.

RAF Museum Library, Hendon

Index

Locators in *italics* refer to illustrations